CU00662155

BWIA'S FIRST FEMALE

Wendy Yawching

We are optimistic about the new strategic direction of BWIA. The changes that are taking place are positive and timely.

We've been shown a future that we can believe in. And that will make all the difference in the world!

Anyone boarding a BWee plane, immediately feels a sense of coming "home" to the Caribbean. For years, our warmth, colour and uniqueness have made us the only true

Caribbean Airline. And that's where we want to stay!

Share The Vision

Courtesy BWIA International/Caribbean Airlines

THE **COURAGE** TO **FLY**

*How to Follow Your Dreams and
Reach for the Sky,
No Matter What the World Tells You*

Special FREE Bonus Gift for You

To help you to fly even higher, there are
FREE BONUS RESOURCES
for you at:

www.FreeGift.theCourage2Fly.com

* Free TheCourage2Fly e-workbook/journal
Special Discount & VIP upgrade to Wendy's signature
transformational workshop, *New Beginnings:
The Ultimate Energy Vision Board Experience*

Wendy Yawching

The Courage to Fly © 2022 Wendy Yawching

All rights reserved. No part of this book may be
reproduced or used in any manner without the
prior written permission of the copyright owner,
except for the use of brief quotations in a book review.

To request permissions, contact: **www.theCourage2Fly.com**

Paperback ISBN: 979-8-218-06723-6
E-book eISBN: 979-8-218-07915-4

Edited by: **Darby Maloney**
Cover design by: **Sehar**
Layout by: **Print on Demand Ltd.**
Photographs by: **B.W.I.A. Archives, Wendy Yawching Archives and F. Hosein.**

Publisher:
Wendy Yawching, Healing Spaces Caribbean
Trinidad and Tobago, W.I.

Publisher's website: **www.theCourage2Fly.com**

Printed by:
Print on Demand Ltd., 79 Tragarete Road, Trinidad and Tobago, W.I.

First Edition

WHAT OTHERS ARE SAYING ABOUT
WENDY YAWCHING
&
THE COURAGE TO FLY

"As I pored over Wendy Yawching's book, it became apparent that ours was a shared mission: one to empower women and girls. 'The Courage to Fly' goes beyond being a well-written and engaging autobiography in which the author has the audacity to challenge what is perceived to be a man's world. It is a lesson to all women and girls that not only must you make your dreams a reality but, once you embark on life's journey, the sky is no limit. The book is a must read for all young women who have a dream. Let your life be a message to the world. Let it be inspiring."

—**Sharon Clark-Rowley,** LLB, LEC, partner M.G Daly & Partners, Wife of the Prime Minister of Trinidad and Tobago

"Riveting, powerful, inspirational, motivational, a must read for all. Captain Wendy Yawching shares her courageous, amazing and until now, enigmatic, guarded, almost controversial life. 'The Courage to Fly' tells the story of a fearless, legendary, adventurous, eco-warrior woman who finally reveals her life's struggles and journey, in a time and period when girls should not dream of being in a boys' world, when a small island Caribbean girl should not dare challenge the international realm. Yet she persevered, and conquered . . . achieving her dreams in a challenging and unforgiving era. Captain Wendy emphatically says, and has proven: Yes, you can . . . any age, any gender, any nationality, anytime. ***Dreams Do Come True!***"

—**Fareeda Hosein,** Managing Director, Darkroom Designs, Print on Demand Ltd., Trinidad/Tobago

"Thirty years ago, I had the enormous privilege to recognize Captain Wendy's talent and her courage to succeed. She was one of 80 successful women to be featured in my book "Why Not A Woman", a pioneer lighting the way forward. Her book, 'The Courage to Fly', is a must have for every woman and girl. Her generosity in sharing her story, one of ups and downs, stick-to-itiveness, determination and motivation… will be an inspiration to all who are on the journey and who might need a little encouragement. And yes, men can read the book too!!"

—**Radhica Saith,** Executive Producer "Why not a Woman"

"Engaging, enlightening and empowering, this offering is an enthralling combination of professional insight and personal testimonial. Captain Wendy shares the highlights and pitfalls of an impressive career, going where few women 'have gone before'. She is to be congratulated for this achievement delivered with characteristic strength of conviction, generosity and grace. This is a book to be shared with current and future generations!"

—**Alissandra Cummins,** Director,
Barbados Museum and Historical Society

"A book about achieving excellence and trailblazing, character, ambition, and finding your way. It is sure to inspire anyone with a dream, especially one that defies cultural and/or family norms. Wendy Yawching is a true renaissance woman."

—**Marnie Landon,** Founder/CEO,
C 2 Infinity corp. Canada

"Captain Wendy's journey is an absolute inspiration that can lead women and girls to a place of wonder and a life of curiosity blended with freedom. Courage looks like this!"

—**Nicole Joseph-Chin,** Social Entrepreneur and
Women's Health Advocate

"For the many years I have known Wendy Yawching she has always been quite private about her career as a pilot. Imagine my surprise when she announced she was writing a book about her journey. Once again, she put her fears and doubts aside and plunged forward with all her heart and soul to share her story with you. Wendy felt strongly she had something of value to share with all those who are in doubt or fear about their aspirations and dreams, who wonder Can I? Will I? May I? She is here now with these pages to say with utmost assuredness, Yes you can, yes you may and YES YOU WILL. Her courage, perseverance and belief in herself brought this book to fruition so you may glean from her experience The Courage to Fly. May her wings carry you forth to greatness."

— **Marjorie Linglet,** *USA*

"This book is a MUST read for anyone who has ever had a dream that everyone else said was unattainable, for anyone who might be thinking that it's too late in life to switch gears and make a career change. Wendy Yawching successfully conquered both feats and guides the reader on how they too can achieve the same. She is an amazing teacher, mentor, trailblazer, friend, confidant, but of the many hats worn by Wendy, "Captain" has been the one that she is most well known for in her native country of Trinidad and Tobago. Now, she shares with the world at large what it took for her to live her dreams and create her best life in this curated, heartwarming, inspiring collection of personal stories each with a special life lesson."

—**Terri Osborne,** Visual Storyteller, Trinidad/Tobago

"In the 30+ years I have known Wendy , she has demonstrated time and time again her amazing ability to manifest her dreams no matter what anyone thought. This book should serve as an inspiration to anyone who chooses a different path or who is told it can't be done. Being a pioneer takes hard work and determination, but it is not out of reach for anyone who dares. Wendy's story may seem fantastical in a time when women enjoy so many freedoms and choices, but it is on the shoulders of women like Wendy and many others that the "modern woman" stands, and we should never forget how far we have indeed come. I hope that Wendy's story inspires others to dream their best selves and let nothing stand in their way".

—**Reshma Saith** BA MBA, LL.b, LEC, USA

"Amazing, illuminating and inspiring. Wendy is a wonderfully insightful teacher of the important things of life."

—**Jenny Pasquini,** UK

"'The Courage to Fly' isn't one of those books that merely encourages women to follow their dreams. Oh, no. Author Wendy Yawching doesn't just talk the talk; she walks the walk, and her firsthand experience makes an electrifying difference.

Society in the 70s expected—no, demanded—that females pursue traditional roles. Unfazed and against the odds, Yawching followed her unconventional dream of becoming a jet pilot. She describes the hurdles she overcame through determination, hard work, and struggle to become a captain. The underlying revelation she feels compelled to share is simple: Girls. Can. Do. Anything. Each chapter ends with a message and tips that reinforce this theme.

Despite the book's targeting females, males will find lots to intrigue them in this comprehensive inside look at what's involved in becoming a jet pilot. Readers' only complaint will be that they'll wish the book was longer."

—**Jeanne Mason,** editor and author
(Casey Jones: American Hero; Sixteen; Trinidad Noir and other titles), USA

"Captain Wendy takes you on an incredible journey in 'The Courage To Fly' that
only a female pilot and legend in her field can, while lighting the fire in you to write
your own rules and pursue the extraordinary. Her witty voice in the recounting of
her life as a pilot is captivating, honest, inspiring and filled with never before heard
stories from the cockpit, and the real life of one of the most important and inspiring
women I have the honour of knowing."
                    —**First Officer Shannon Hutchinson**, Airline Pilot, Canada

"Every opportunity I've had to learn from Wendy Yawching has opened my eyes
to seeing so much in the typically unseen aspects of myself. She has helped me to
achieve the life I truly envision and I am confident that her approach can help you
thrive too!"
                         —**Dr Keisha Abraham**, President, Abraham Agency, USA

"Wendy's book is a little gem written by a big gem of the Caribbean. She has shown
courage, strength, pioneer-ship along with sensitivity and wisdom. As she travels
into her golden years Wendy continues to serve the world. I have known her for 22
years and know that she will do her very best in everything that she does and for
that I honor her. She is a soul sister that I love dearly and wish her all the very best
on her continued journey."
                          —**Dr Sharon Sage,** DO,ND, Bsc(Hons) OST Med, DVM
                                                                          Grenada

"For me, Wendy Yawching is synonymous with courage. She is the embodiment of
what courage looks like . . . regardless of our age and stage of development. Every
young Caribbean woman should read this book to gain the courage to discover and
spread her own wings. 'The Courage to Fly' serves to remind us all, that courage
isn't found in the skies . . . but it's what gets us there . . . one choice at a time.
As Wendy so elegantly shows us . . . we can choose courage."
                     —**Penelope Camps,** Founder & CEO, Yahweh Foundation Tobago.

"Once I started reading this book, I could not stop. This is a very emotive, written
from the heart, inspiring story of a determined young woman . . . determined to
stand firm, to be true to herself, the follow the call of her spirit, to make her dreams
happen. Wendy Yawching brings her experiences to us without fear; sharing the
good, the not so good and the heartbreaking, so that girls and women who read this
memoir will find their own courage to fly."
          —**Vidya Lall,** Senior Instructor, University of Trinidad & Tobago (UTT)

DEDICATION

I dedicate this book to my family.

You are the roots of my life ... from you I gained

the strength and courage to fly with my own wings.

Phyllis Yawching (Mum)

Claude Yawching (Dad)

Donna and Dexter Yawching (my Indian-Chief siblings)

Kemlan Yawching (Step-Mom and maker of the best apple-crumble in the world)

I love you all.

DISCLAIMER AND/OR LEGAL NOTICES While all attempts have been made to verify information provided in this book and its ancillary materials, neither the author or publisher assumes any responsibility for errors, inaccuracies or omissions and is not responsible for any financial loss by customer in any manner. Any slights of people or organizations are unintentional. If advice concerning legal, financial, accounting or related matters is needed, the services of a qualified professional should be sought. This book and its associated ancillary materials, including verbal and written training, is not intended for use as a source of legal, financial or accounting advice. You should be aware of the various laws governing business transactions or other business practices in your particular geographical location.

EARNINGS & INCOME DISCLAIMER With respect to the reliability, accuracy, timeliness, usefulness, adequacy, completeness, and/ or suitability of information provided in this book, Wendy Yawching, Healing Spaces Caribbean, its partners, associates, affiliates, consultants, and/or presenters make no warranties, guarantees, representations, or claims of any kind. Readers' results will vary depending on a number of factors. Any and all claims or representations as to income earnings are not to be considered as average earnings. Testimonials are not representative. This book and all products and services are for educational and informational purposes only. Use caution and see the advice of qualified professionals. Check with your accountant, attorney or professional advisor before acting on this or any information. You agree that Wendy Yawching, Healing Spaces Caribbean, is/ are not responsible for the success or failure of your personal, business, health or financial decisions relating to any information presented by Wendy Yawching, Healing Spaces Caribbean or company products/services. Earnings potential is entirely dependent on the efforts, skills and application of the individual person. Any examples, stories, references, or case studies are for illustrative purposes only and should not be interpreted as testimonies and/or examples of what reader and/or consumers can generally expect from the information. No representation in any part of this information, materials and/or seminar training are guarantees or promises for actual performance. Any statements, strategies, concepts, techniques, exercises and ideas in the information, materials and/or seminar training offered are simply opinion or experience, and thus should not be misinterpreted as promises, typical results or guarantees (expressed or implied). The author and publisher (Wendy Yawching, Healing Spaces Caribbean or any of their representatives) shall in no way, under any circumstances, be held liable to any party (or third party) for any direct, indirect, punitive, special, incidental or other consequential damages arising directly or indirectly from any use of books, materials and or seminar trainings, which is provided "as is," and without warranties.

MOTIVATE & INSPIRE OTHERS
Share this Book

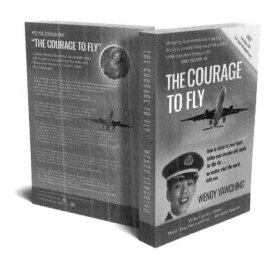

Retail US$21.95

Special Quantity Discount Prices *

5-20 books	$18.95
21-99 books	$15.95
100-499 books	$12.95
500-999 books	$9.95

* Plus applicable Shipping and Handling fees

To Place an Order, contact:
www.books.theCourage2Fly.com

THE IDEAL PROFESSIONAL SPEAKER FOR YOUR NEXT EVENT

Any school, group or organisation that seeks

to help girls and women

to become "extraordinary,"

should hire WENDY YAWCHING

for a keynote and /or workshop training!

TO CONTACT OR BOOK

WENDY YAWCHING

TO SPEAK:

www.speaker.theCourage2Fly.com

AN INSPIRING
COACH or MENTOR

If you're ready to overcome inner obstacles,

have major breakthroughs and soar to higher levels,

then you will love having

WENDY YAWCHING

as your coach or mentor!

TO CONTACT OR BOOK

WENDY YAWCHING

FOR MENTORING/CONSULTING:

www.mentor.theCourage2Fly.com

TABLE OF CONTENTS

PART ONE
BUTTERFLY
1965-1999

CONTENTS continued . . .

PART TWO
EAGLE
1999-2014

CONTENTS continued . . .

PART THREE
HUMMINGBIRD
2007- present (2022)

A MESSAGE TO YOU!

Over the years, lots of people have asked me to write a book about my life adventures, and I resisted for many reasons. First, I've never considered myself a "proper" writer. That honour goes to my older sister Donna, who knows how to turn words into magic. And then, there's this: I've never particularly liked reading autobiographies of other people, even the fascinating ones who changed history. I'd much rather go see the movie!

So the thought of writing an autobiography that probably no one would read (except for my family) seemed not to be worth the time . . . because - and this is the real reason - I've always been so busy living life, there never seems to be time to jot it down. Pictures, sure. Writing? Meh.

And then, quite recently, someone asked me this question: What would you say to your eighteen year old self, if you could go back in time and have a coffee together? I thought about that. Really thought about it. And the idea for this book was born.

You see, if my eighteen year old self had known then, what I've learned with great effort over the decades that separate us . . . I wouldn't have doubted myself for so long, I would not have listened to all the voices that told me "Girls don't do that", and I would not have spent so many years doing things that seemed sensible and "normal".

I would have had the courage to be ME, from the get-go.

Truth be told, I rather love where I'm at and who I am now, so I probably wouldn't change a thing. Well, maybe I *would* change a few things: I would have been bolder, brighter, more confident and daring much earlier! Instead, I had to learn to believe. I had to struggle like a butterfly, to burst out of the chrysalis and open those wings. And I did.

And now, here I am . . . writing that book at last, bringing to YOU a handy little guide that, if OLDER Wendy had sneakily passed through the time-warp to YOUNGER Wendy, might have saved me a whole lot of time and worry and angst and lonely soul-searching and difficult scary choices.

So here it is, my gift to that young beautiful eighteen year old Wendy. I'm now waiting for that hole to open up in the fabric of time so that I can slip it through, or even better walk through myself and have that coffee with her. Eighteen year old me really needed to hear this stuff, to know and believe in it, at the beginning of my adult life.

As I wrote it, I realised that the information in this book could have been useful to me at many checkpoints, or choice points, in my life . . . right up to where I am now. There were so many places and times when these lessons would have helped me to struggle less, to have the confidence to follow my heart without fear.

This book is also my gift to you, to help you navigate the many checkpoints/choice points that will occur in your life, no matter how old (or young) you are.

I hope this book speaks to the child in You.
I hope that it inspires you to live your dream without apology.

Perhaps you're a teenager and overwhelmed with the thought of what's ahead, perhaps afraid to dream big because of the messages from the world and people that surround you . . .

Perhaps you're 30 and looking at life or career changes and hesitating even though your heart is calling for new beginnings . . .
Or in your 40's and feel that your life has become smaller than you expected, you're not living the life you dreamed of . . .
In your 50's and possibly you're looking at an empty nest, or other changes in your life and home . . .
In your 60's and you're facing the transition from your career, and unsure of what to do next.

Whenever, wherever you are in your life ...

This is a book that can help you when you are faced with life choices, and you feel less than adequate to the task, when you have been programmed to stay safe and small but your heart wants to soar.

This is a book for you whenever you need to find 'The Courage to Fly'.

PROLOGUE

Dreams *do* come true.

I t's 3 a.m.

I am wide awake at 33,000 feet, suspended in velvet blackness, looking down at the sleeping world below. Around me are the quiet noises of a big jet airplane at cruise. Multicolored lights, subtly dimmed, the gentle tremble of the metal giant powering through the night sky.

We are about to cross the Eastern Seaboard and head out across the ocean in an almost straight line for the Caribbean, and home.

To my right, the first officer quietly responds to air traffic control, logging our progress through the skies. Straight ahead, we see the flash and fire of a distant thunderstorm. We'll need to ask for a deviation around that one.

To the left, I catch my reflection on the cockpit pane, superimposed upon the dark skies. I gaze beyond and down, at the sparkling city below, jewels in the blackness, and then at the shimmer of the moonlit sea ahead.

I catch my breath because it's all so darned beautiful, so ethereal that I feel this is as close to heaven as I can be and still be alive. In fact (here's something I couldn't tell anyone when I was actively flying but can admit now that I'm retired), sometimes I felt as though I could happily die right there, at 33,000 feet, in the middle of the night . . . because I was in heaven already.

My heart, my soul, love these magnificent magical night flights. My body? Not at all.

By the time I fall into my own bed, the sun will have been up for three hours and I will have been awake for sixteen, at least ten of these performing my duties as captain: staying alert, focused, responsive and responsible through the night while 150 passengers sleep, knowing that whatever happens along the way, all eyes look to me to save the situation. The buck stops here, in the left seat of this jet.

This job can be exhausting. It takes a huge physical and mental toll, and adjusting to the constantly disturbed circadian rhythms is hard for me. And yet . . . I wouldn't trade this life for anything:

> I love being a captain.
> I love that my office is the sky.
> I love going to work, strapping into a big jet and roaring off into the heavens.
> I love the beauty of this wonderful planet and that I get to see it from a whole new perspective.
> I love the challenges inherent in the job, every single day.
> I love knowing that I have been trained to meet those challenges, and that I have the skill and expertise to handle most of them, and the faith to believe that God will handle the ones I can't.
> I love the people who work with me as a team to make each flight the best possible.

Sometimes I feel as though I am the conductor of a talented and well-trained orchestra, each of us working in harmony to make beautiful music, a perfect flight. To be part of this experience is a privilege; I am constantly amazed that I am here, right here, living my dream.

You see, this is the life I dreamed of as a ten-year old Trinidadian girl when no one believed me. The journey here was long, full of hard work and sacrifice, and some good fortune. Now those same people believe in me and are so proud of me. I am "their Captain Wendy," the first female captain of BWIA International (later Caribbean Airlines), Trinidad and Tobago's national airline.

How did I ever get here? I wonder, even as I look around the cockpit and thrill to the magic that runs through me still, after all these years.

It's a long story, and I am about to share some of it with you.

Before I do, I ask that you give me your heart, your imagination, your trust . . . because I will be sharing mine with you . . . no holds barred.

For the first step in our journey together, I want you to write these words down:

❖

Dreams
Do
Come
True

PART ONE

BUTTERFLY
1965-1999

"The Universe and the Light of the Stars come through me."

Rumi

At 3 years old in 1958, nicknamed "Fatso".

CHAPTER 1

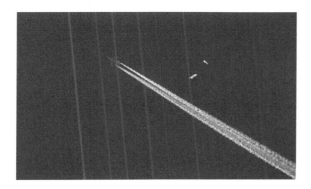

Girls. Don't. Do. That.

I magine this . . .

A little girl, ten years old, lies on the grass looking up at a brilliant blue, almost cloudless sky . . .

Way up high, a jet carves its way through the blue, its twin white contrails streaming out behind, hanging wide for a few minutes—then, slowly, dissipating into nothingness. In an instant, her childhood dreams of becoming a prima ballerina and a park ranger in Africa raising lions and tigers and leopards as pets . . . vaporize like the contrails into thin air.

From that moment, she knows.
She wants to do THAT; she wants to make those trails in the sky.
She wants to fly airplanes, high up there.
She wants to be a pilot.

Imagine this little girl excitedly sharing her new dream with the people she loves most:

Her mum (gently reproachful): "A what? Honey, girls don't do things like that.
I thought you said you wanted to be a ballerina."

Her dad: "Don't worry, Fatso (her family nickname), you'll grow out of it. Girls don't fly planes."

Imagine hearing the same message from everyone in her little world of siblings, extended family, best friends, school pals, teachers, and counsellors. They all agree on one important, immutable fact:

Girls don't do that.

Their words vary—

"A pilot? Get real, that ain't ever going to happen. You ever heard of a girl flying planes?"

"Who would ever hire a lady pilot?"

"I'd never fly on a plane if a girl was in the cockpit!"

—but their message always the same:

GIRLS. DON'T. DO. THAT.

Imagine this little girl, now a teenager, keeping her dream locked inside her heart for fear of ridicule. Eventually, in the ongoing rush of teenage studies and activities, the bright dream fades to an undercurrent, a shadow in her heart. In time she accepts the world that she lives in and her role in it *as defined by the people in her life*. Perhaps they are right. She *should* get real. Perhaps girls DON'T fly planes. Over time, she releases those childhood fantasies and settles into a path that leads to someone else's idea of how she should live her life . . .

Of course, this little girl was me.
But I have a feeling you also know this little girl, in your own life.

Before proceeding, I should explain that all this happened a long time ago.
I was born in 1955 (yes, truly), and the Trinidad in which I grew up was very different from the Trinidad of today. Our home had no TV; the Internet hadn't been invented yet, and smart phones didn't exist. No way could I Google "are there any female pilots."

At ten years old, to me Trinidad and Tobago *was* the world. My view of that world was shaped by those around me: my family, friends and teachers. Our society had strong cultural norms, and the people I looked to for guidance had clear views about the roles of boys and girls:

Boys did "Boy stuff" and girls did "Girl stuff."

At that time, the general expectation was that a girl would graduate from high school, get an acceptable job, and wait for the opportunity to marry, become a homemaker, and start a family. A female who went on to attain a university degree was a rare bird and viewed as a "modern woman." Even so, certain careers were considered acceptable for her; flying airplanes was not one of them.

In my little island world, no one understood this passionate dream of mine. No one in my life flew airplanes or even talked about flying airplanes. No one would encourage such a crazy idea.

So you can imagine the consternation and disbelief when I voiced my burning desire to be a pilot! The news fell like a rock into the quiet pond of my life. I could just as easily have said I wanted to fly to the moon. All the responses (Every. Single. One.) made it absolutely clear:

Girls Don't Fly Airplanes.

When you hear the same message over and over and over from everyone in your life, you begin to wonder if they may be right. You begin to doubt, and eventually, you believe them. That's what happened to me. The flame in my heart still lingered, but I no longer believed that I could ever be a pilot. Girls in my world didn't do Boy stuff, and flying an airplane was definitely considered Boy stuff . . .

I graduated from high school in 1973. Everyone expected me to continue on to university since I was a model student with impressive grades, but financially, tertiary education was not an option. To attend university, I would have to pay my own way, which meant finding a job.

After three months working as a bank teller (definitely not a good fit for me), I joined BWIA, Trinidad and Tobago's national airline, as a flight attendant. No one discouraged me. In fact, everyone agreed that this was an excellent job—for a girl.

For my part, I ran joyously toward this new career, thinking that since I couldn't be a pilot, being a flight attendant might be the next best thing. At least I would be *onboard* an airplane. I would get to know real pilots, hear their stories, visit the cockpit, and live vicariously. I would be a flight attendant whose heart lay beyond the closed cockpit door, even as she served in the cabin.

Being a flight attendant offered other attractions: travel, exciting destinations, learning new skills, meeting lots of people. Yes, becoming a flight attendant would open up a whole new world for me — and I would be closer to those contrails.

A Message for You

You are . . . whatever you believe you are.

CHAPTER 2

Wendy as a flight attendant with BWIA 1973-1976

Girls Can Do ANYTHING

I spent the next three years flying the skies as a flight attendant, diligently serving passengers in the main cabin while wondering about that *other* world, the one behind the closed doors of the cockpit.

For someone who attended a high school run by Catholic nuns where order, structure and proper behavior were required for success, becoming a flight attendant was like letting a bird out of a cage. Here now was a world of unlimited freedoms, new experiences, travel, exciting new friends. In many ways, these years served as an intensive finishing school for me. I learned the art of personal style, acquired a touch of sophistication, and developed strong people management skills. Along the way, I gained a lifelong appreciation for just how much expertise resides behind the smile of a cabin attendant, the rigorous and regular emergency training; and the standards of excellence demanded under pressure.

As my world expanded, I realized that, while female pilots were extremely rare, in some countries women *did* fly planes; but I had long lost the belief that flying a plane was something I could ever do myself. My plan was to proceed to university as soon as I saved enough for a start. My older sister Donna lived in Canada, so that sounded like good place for me.

Hmmm . . . Whatever should I study?

As everyone in my circle reminded me, I was great at math, and there was a new field called computer science which was expected to take over the world; so why not study computer science and set myself up for a really good career? (Apparently computer science was on the list of acceptable female options).

And so it was. In 1976, I departed Trinidad for my new life as a freshman at University of Waterloo in Ontario, which I'd chosen because of its great computer science program. I had enough money to get started and keep me going for eight months, after which I would need to work to support myself for the remainder of the program.

Almost five years later, I graduated with a BSc in Math and Computer Science . . . and the realization that they were wrong. They were ALL wrong.

Girls could do ANYTHING they wanted to do.

That, my friend, was the single most important thing I learned at university.

During those years, I saw girls driving huge trucks and backhoes and wearing boots and hard hats and working on construction sites alongside men.

I met girls studying to be electricians, plumbers, engineers, architects, lawyers, and neuroscientists, and they were not expected to marry at twenty and give it all up—unless *they* chose to.

My university roommate was the head of the (mostly male) engineering society, which was a big deal—*and* she had been voted in by the men.

I learned that girls could go camping together in the wild, hoist canoes on their heads, survive on berries for a week—and call it fun.

Actually, the first time I tried camping, it rained for three days, and was the most awful, cold, wet, uncomfortable experience in my life— one I resolved never to repeat—until the fourth day when the sun came out. Everything changed, and the remainder of the trip became the most beautiful, sparkling, fun adventure I had ever experienced. This marked the start of my lifelong love affair with the outdoors and nature.

None of these pursuits were normal for Trinidadian girls at that time, and certainly not in my personal frame of reference . . . until I lived in Canada among girls who didn't see anything unusual about doing whatever they wanted to do with their lives, girls who saw themselves as equal to the guys who surrounded them at university.

Slowly, incredulously, my eyes opened to new possibilities. Best of all, when I voiced my long-buried dream of being a jet pilot, the answer from my Canadian buddies was always:

Go for it!
How cool!
Why Not?
Of course you can!

What a difference.

By this time, I also realized that there were actually *many* female pilots, gainfully employed by airlines in Canada and around the world, even though none in my own country. Trinidad and Tobago had not yet caught up with what was possible for women. Our women weren't lacking potential; the issue was that our society didn't allow them to believe they could do unusual things. In such an environment, stepping outside the lines to create your own story can seem almost impossible.

The idea that a woman can do or be anything she desires may seem obvious to you, because you have the benefit of having grown up in a different time. For me, it was a HUGE realization, a quantum shift of my internal compass..

Indeed, I *did* learn a lot at University of Waterloo—and what I learned had little to do with my computer science degree.

Oh, Canada! You changed my life. You saved my life.

You taught me that if I was willing to put in the work, I could be anything I wanted. I could be a ballerina, a park ranger with lions and tigers and leopards as pets . . . or a jet pilot. You showed me that

GIRLS. CAN. DO. ANYTHING.

And that's why, newly graduated at twenty-six, I made up my mind. Instead of flying home to Trinidad to that great computer science job, I would stay in Canada and train to become a pilot.

A Message for You
*Never listen to other people who tell you what you **can't** do.*
Instead, listen to your heart.

CHAPTER 3

My Pilot Journey Begins
(I can, I will, watch me)

After all those years of yearning, of wishing, of being discouraged by others, my passion now swelled until it erupted in a crashing wave of certainty.
I would go for it.
I would learn to fly.
One day, I WOULD be a pilot.

Instead of returning home, I informed my shocked parents that I needed to stay in Canada and learn to fly airplanes. There was just one little problem.

The cost of flying lessons was astronomical (even more so nowadays). After five years of studying and working to support my education, my funds were almost zero. My parents could not help financially, and I had no rich relatives. Financing my flying lessons would be up to me. Hmmm, this would need some thought . . . but I was committed to my path.

I soon discovered an excellent local institution that offered a three-year degree program in Aviation and Flight Technology, and, for their top thirty students—free flight training to the level of commercial pilot. Aha! This was just what I needed! The opportunity was amazing. Thousands applied to the program, approximately one hundred were chosen to start, and at the end of the first year, the top thirty were selected to proceed to flight training.

I applied among that field of thousands and was accepted. I worked my butt off, made it through that crucial first year at the top of my class, and was chosen to enter Year 2. Free flight training ahead!
Except that's not how my story goes.

Within weeks of starting the second year and with flight training imminent, I realized something was wrong. Each morning I felt ill, stressed and panicked at the very thought of going to school.
How could this be? Becoming a pilot was my dream! Why wasn't I happy?
My boyfriend suggested I seek help, and I bless him for it.

Within one session, my psychotherapist pinpointed the problem. Apparently, the first intense year had affected me psychologically. I was experiencing a form of stress disorder from the intensity of the program and the high level of competition required.

When I walked out of the therapist's office, I felt like a light had come on within me. His assessment made such sense. I had never been competitive before, always preferring the cooperative approach where each person helps the others to rise. Yet I had just spent the last year in a heads-down, no-holds-barred competition with one hundred students to ensure that I would be among the thirty candidates chosen. Such an approach was totally against my nature, and my body, mind, and spirit were rebelling against it.

Despite the bright lure of free flight training, I resolved to find another way to reach my dream. I quit the program.

I have never been a quitter, so everyone in my life registered huge shock and disbelief. But I knew in my heart this matter was one of personal well-being. Of survival. As determined as ever, I now had to find employment that would support my very expensive habit.

Armed with my university certificate, I searched for work in the computer field. In those days, computers were huge standing giants kept in large, temperature-controlled rooms, and attended to by computer programmers who spoke their jargon.

I landed a job at an insurance company that needed someone personable who could act as intermediary between their programmers and the insurance professionals who needed data (from those scary computer banks presented in ways they could understand). I was that person! The job was perfect for someone with my skillset: computer knowledge combined with excellent people skills honed by my years as a flight attendant. I enjoyed the work, and it just about paid for my flight training. Even more important was that my boss allowed me flexible hours so I could fly several times a week.

For three years, I worked full-time at the insurance company and spent every free moment training at Buttonville Airport, just north of Toronto. Because my flying lessons gobbled up a shocking amount of money, my two credit cards were constantly maxed. To make it through, I gave up most of my social life, choosing to stay home watching TV with a simple home-cooked dinner instead of going out to a movie with friends. I could afford only the basics; I had no money for extras.

Each milestone was a delight and a personal triumph:

First solo flight:	Check. *What a rush!*
Private pilot's license:	Check. *This meant I could invite my friends to fly with me in a little Cessna 150—and give them a good scare.*
Commercial pilot's license:	Check. *This meant I could apply for a paid flying job.*

I had just one little problem . . . with the ink barely dried on my licenses and no experience in the real flying world, no airline would hire me. So I decided to become an instructor. More training, more studying, more money, more exams. Then:

Instructor rating:	Check. *Now I could get a job teaching beginners how to fly.*

That's how, in 1984, I became a flying instructor at Central Airways, located at Toronto Island's pretty little airport.

Unfortunately, new pilot instructors didn't make much money; employers knew that we were teaching in order to build up flight hours to become attractive to the big airlines. To survive, I needed another income. So for the next two years, I worked six-and-a-half days per week every week: three-and-a-half days teaching beginners to fly (loved it), and three days as a computer freelancer (to pay the bills). That left half a day to do laundry, groceries, and get some rest before starting the week all over again.

Years later, people would see me stride across the airport in my full uniform and think *Oh my God, how lucky she is!* They have no idea. My success was NOT mere luck; it was years of dedication, determination, hard work, and struggle.

I FOLLOWED MY DREAM WITH ALL MY HEART.

They say *God helps those who help themselves;* I trusted in that maxim. And yes— there *was* a bit of luck in there, too.

A Message for You

Whether you think you can or think you can't, you're right.

—Henry Ford

CHAPTER 4

A *Real* Pilot

The year was 1986, and I was leaving Canada after residing there for a decade. I was heading back to the Caribbean to live in Antigua and fly for LIAT. I had landed my first "real" flying job with a real airline! The past few months were a crazy blur in my mind. Everything in my life had changed, all because of a blizzard.

One day in mid-December 1985, I was instructing a new student in the airspace east of Toronto when I got this radio call:

COME BACK NOW!

I raced back to Toronto Island Airport against an approaching storm that was closing in much earlier than forecast. As the blizzard hit the airport, I landed the Cessna 150 in almost whiteout conditions with big fat flurries whipping horizontally across the windscreen.

We were the last aircraft in. As soon as we touched down, they closed the airfield. Everyone still flying out there would have to land somewhere else. The visibility was so poor we could not safely taxi back to the hanger, so wing-walkers were sent out to bring us in.

As I defrosted in the warmth of the lounge, I thought about the dangers of flying a tiny airplane with no deicing equipment in such weather. I recalled my boyfriend's recent words:

> "You know you're getting older, right?"

> I was newly thirty.

> "You know most pilot-hires are twenty-one or twenty-two years old, right?"

> I knew this. Most had rich dads who could pay for flight training right out of high school.

> "Wendy, if you're serious about being a real pilot, stop wasting time and get out there!"

By "real" pilot and "out there," he meant stepping up to the bigger leagues and flying for an airline with more sophisticated aircraft. That early winter blizzard was the kicker that made me pause and think deeply. Canada had been very good to me, but I hated the long dark winters; my tropical soul yearned for more sunshine in my life. I had been an instructor for 2 years and I loved it; but I was still far away from my childhood dream of flying the big jets.

There was only one way to get to that dream of mine. The time had come to move on.

I contacted my old employer BWIA, who happened to have recently hired their first female pilot. Apparently things had changed a lot in Trinidad since my departure ten years earlier. BWIA was glad to hear from me, but they weren't planning to hire any more pilots for another two years.

Two years! I couldn't afford to wait so long. You see, in the aviation world I was already considered ancient. As my boyfriend so kindly pointed out, most new pilots are in their early twenties, yet here I was at thirty looking for my first airline job.

Never one to give up easily, I reached out to LIAT, the smaller regional airline based in Antigua that serviced the Caribbean islands. LIAT was hiring, but they required the same licenses and ratings as BWIA, which meant getting a multi-IFR rating* and converting my Canadian licenses to the British equivalent, since aviation in the Caribbean still operated under British law at that time.

LIAT told me to contact them as soon as I got the necessaries. That was all I needed to hear. To quote a famous movie, I told them, "I'll be back!"

Brave words, indeed.

I considered the challenges ahead: The multi-engine IFR rating was prohibitively expensive, which was why I hadn't done it earlier. The British Airline Transport Pilot Licence (the highest pilot's qualification available at that time) was infamous as being the toughest set of written examinations of all and had been known to make grown men cry. Many Trinidadian pilots had attempted to study for these exams at home, tutored by a local instructor. Many failed on their first and even second attempts. My best chance for success was to study in England at a recognized flying school, but living in the UK for months would be terribly expensive.

I had no idea how I was going to pull this off financially. I did have a little savings, but when that was gone, I would have to depend on my two trusty credit cards. Success was not guaranteed, and neither was my being hired at the end of this journey. I might never be able to pay off my bills. I was heading into a financial tsunami—but I didn't care. I was determined to make it happen.

---

* Multi-IFR rating: qualification to fly an airplane with more than one engine, under instrument flight rules.

Within a week I was in Florida, starting the journey to obtaining my multi-engine rating on a beautiful twin-engine Cessna 310. As soon as I had that certification in hand, I rushed back to Toronto, packed my cold weather bags, and flew off to England to do the British conversion training and exams.

Thus began two months of the hardest studying I have ever done. What made it bearable was the camaraderie of our training group. I was the only female in a group of thirty male pilots, and we all helped each other. Before we knew it, the incredibly challenging exams were upon us, behind us— and I had passed with flying colors! British license, check!

When I contacted LIAT, they didn't hesitate: The job was mine. Report for Ground School in Antigua next Monday.

I had six days to wrap up my life in Canada. I was leaving behind a promising computer career, my clients, my flying students, and a lot of friends who thought I was crazy. But, as you understand by now, I didn't have a choice—not *really*.

I was thirty years old and off to start a new career with no guarantee that I would succeed.

I was going to be a real pilot.

A Message for You

Achieving amazing things is probably never going to be easy— but it's so worth the journey!

CHAPTER 5

LIAT Twin Otter, 1986

Living the Dream

2005.

| Air Traffic Control (ATC): | "West Indian 521, contact San Juan Center 132 decimal 15; goodnight." |
| Captain Wendy: | "San Juan Center 132 decimal 15, have a good night. West Indian 521." |

Entering Caribbean airspace; another hour to landing and home.

The night sky begins to lighten in the East; fingers of rosy dawn sneak over the horizon, creating a surreal changing canvas . . . then there's that unbelievably beautiful moment when I can see the moon shining in the darkness through the first officer's window and the rising sun and pearly clouds glowing through my own window, as if this big jet is suspended between two magical worlds.

Looking down at the little island of Antigua, I remember living there from 1986 to 1988 working for LIAT, years in which I really learned to fly; those two happy years that took a rookie and made her a *pilot*.

I remember the first day the LIAT trainers walked us new pilots through the hangars. I thought I had never seen anything so big or beautiful as the De Havilland Twin Otter aircraft that we were going to train on. Nineteen seats! Wow! Until now, the biggest plane I had flown had four seats. As we say in the Caribbean, "Ah reach!"

The Twin Otter was the smaller of LIAT's two aircraft types and did all the small island hopping throughout the Caribbean. After weeks of training, I was qualified to operate as a first officer on the Otter, flying from the right seat. The captain, in command of the entire operation, sat next to me in the left seat.

Many people don't realize that both pilots in the cockpit are fully qualified pilots who take turns flying the aircraft. Having two pilots makes perfect sense: If something happens to one pilot there is always someone up there who knows what to do! The difference between pilots lies in rank and experience, the captain having the senior rank and the most experience.

A typical flying day involved landing at eight tiny airports, each with its special challenges. Many of those runways started at the base of a hill, and ended at the sea. Touching down in exactly the right place and stopping before the blue is critical. You could never take it for granted, no matter how many times you'd landed there.

Sharing some memories with you:

Carriacou: ATC* would often say "Cleared to land, look out for cows on the runway."

*Air Traffic Control

Union Island, our approach technique: Fly straight at the hill, look for the house with the blue roof, turn a hard right over their laundry line, and dive to the runway.

St. Barts: Fly as low as you can over the hill with all the crosses (marking dead people). Then dive down to the runway and watch out for the sea at the end.

St Eustatius: A long runway, but there just happens to be a large volcano off to the right side. When the winds are strong, they come over this volcano and get all excited, roiling and rolling and churning across the first part of the runway. Look out for windshear!

But the most exciting of all was Cane Field, Dominica.

The prevailing winds in the Caribbean are from the East, and most runways are laid to align as much as possible with these winds. Because of Dominica's topography, the runway was laid north-south along a small strip of flat land on the west coast. At each end of the short runway was a little hill. Behind the runway were towering hills with the wind rolling down them. I have never experienced such exciting landings as at Cane Field! The pilots used to say, "When Cane Field kicking, brave men weep."

During my first year at LIAT, the airline had their first (and only) crash. The accident happened at night in bad weather at St Vincent, another airfield that required huge respect. The first officer was a new pilot like me, and we were friends. In fact, I was supposed to pick him up after his flight since he had not yet bought a car. I will never forget the moment I understood that he was never coming home.

At the time, I was the third female pilot at LIAT. The other two women were senior to me and captains on the Twin Otter. The guys, who were a mix of nationalities from the various islands, treated me with a blend of humor and machismo. They soon realized I was keen to learn and devised challenges to test me and improve my flying skills.

After ten years of winter, I really enjoyed living in Antigua. When I was not flying, my life felt like one big holiday of sun, sea, and sky filled with outdoor adventures and good friends. I made it my personal goal to visit every single Caribbean island. Each month, I organized a few days off and jump-seated† to a small island to explore. By the time I left Antigua, I had visited almost every island from Trinidad to Puerto Rico, including some tiny ones that most people don't know about. Every island is unique, and I enjoyed getting to know the nuances of each one.

At some point, I was promoted to the beautiful fifty-seater De Havilland Dash 8, brand new and high tech at the time, and very sophisticated when compared to the Twin Otter. I was in heaven!

My routes were now different. We flew to the "bigger" airports, including Puerto Rico, Barbados, and Trinidad. No more the excitement of Union Island or Cane Field, but this lovely new airplane was excitement enough for me.

My LIAT years were years of learning, exhilaration, and fun.
I learned to handle an airplane under tough conditions, a skill that has served me well.
I learned to work as part of a team—no matter who was sitting next to me.
I learned to respect the weather and the airfields.
I learned to never take anything about flying for granted but to check and double check.
I learned firsthand about Murphy's Law.

I learned to respect and appreciate the many people who made our flights possible: the ground staff, engineers, mechanics, fuelers, and baggage handlers. We were part of a functioning organism, and no part could survive without the other parts doing their job well.
And I loved it all.
I was happy.

Then, in 1988, I got two calls, one from BWIA and one from Air Canada.

† a wonderful perk of the job: flying for free, sitting in the extra cockpit seat.

Both were ready for me.

Air Canada offered me a job in Winnipeg (think -40 Celsius in winter).

BWIA was based in Trinidad.

Guess which I chose.

A Message for You

Don't be afraid to reach for the stars,
if you do fall, you may land on the moon

CHAPTER 6

Flying the Big Jets

After twelve years abroad, imagine my joy and excitement at returning to my first airline, BWIA— not as a cabin attendant, but as a jet pilot! My dream had come true; I was now a first officer on the MD83 jet, the airline's first woman *ever* to be in a flying position. The female pilot that had been hired before me was still in a non-flying position as a flight engineer (aka third pilot) on the transatlantic jets.

Everyone was watching me. The jury was out concerning my success. I *had* to excel—both for myself and for future female pilots.

The MD83, which could seat approximately 150 passengers, served BWIA's medium-haul routes throughout the Caribbean and North and South America. Among pilots, the MD83 was known as "a pilot's airplane": sleek, maneuverable—and unforgiving. The word was that if you didn't know how to fly the MD83 properly, that jet would fly you, making your short-comings embarrassingly clear. People waited to see how I would fare on such a beast, and I was determined to show that I was up to the challenge.

Despite the pressure to prove my worth as a pilot, I loved everything about my new job: the months of training, the simulator challenges, the speed and power of flying a jet. I was insatiable, and found it hard to believe that I was being paid to do something that made me so happy.

Did I have difficult moments? Oh, yes. I'll never forget my first route check, the final challenge to complete my initial training . . .

Very much a newbie—armed with theory and simulator success but not much else—I was to be examined on a normal passenger flight by one of the most feared check captains of the day. His nickname was "Shaka Zulu,"* which will give you some idea of his reputation! I couldn't sleep the night before my flight, trembling in fear of this great man in whose hands my flying career rested.

The next day, Shaka Zulu followed me closely through all the preflight procedures, asking question after question. To my dismay, after passengers boarded, we found a mechanical issue and had to swap airplanes. I had to do the preflight all over again on another aircraft, with him at my side watching my every move and asking technical questions.

I was thankful that this new plane checked out fine. We departed a couple of hours late on our planned route: Barbados, Antigua, Jamaica.

Shaka Zulu sat in the jump-seat scrutinizing my movements, listening to every word, and making frequent notes. On arrival in Antigua, we had another technical problem (Murphy's law!). After the engineers investigated, we were instructed to disembark all of our passengers and ferry the empty airplane back home with the landing gear down. This was a new situation for me—and one that we'd never practiced in simulator training.

*African tribal leader sometimes compared with Attila the Hun.

I remember doing the performance calculations by hand for flying with the gear down, with Shaka Zulu watching and checking everything I did. Through the entire flight back to Trinidad with the landing gear down, he kept making notes.

When we finally landed in Trinidad, Flight Operations informed us that we were required to take yet another aircraft to Jamaica for the waiting crew and southbound passengers who would otherwise be stranded there. *Here we go again: my third pre-flight for the day!*

At that point, Shaka Zulu turned to me. "I've seen enough, I'm going home now. You're fine." Then he picked up his bag and left us to fly to Jamaica without him.

I don't think there has ever been another route check quite like that one. From that day, my fear of Shaka Zulu melted into respect. He took me under his wing and spent our many flights together teaching me the million things that make a good pilot.

As a first officer, I was like a sponge, soaking up all the advice, training, and experience that came my way. I learned never to take anything on a flight for granted, but rather to check and double check. I learned that I loved the challenge of operating into high density airports (like JFK), and that part of me thrills when a situation needs extra skill and expertise, since that's when all our training pays off.

Over time, I learned that the captain is not God nor infallible, and that my input was important; so I learned to assert myself when needed, in an appropriate and timely manner. That way, the captain and I became a highly functioning two-person team!

Outside the cockpit, I learned that, despite the "glamour" and respect our profession brings, we are wingless without a huge extended team. The integrity of a flight depends on many people doing their job to perfection: mechanics, baggage handlers, load sheet agents, flight operations team, and the flight attendants. (By the way, always respect your flight attendants; they're the ones who are going to get you out of that downed airplane safely, and they're the only ones who actually know how to work all that survival equipment.) I learned to value all of these people. My life was literally in their hands, as the passengers' lives were in ours.

Did I have scary moments? Another yes. I experienced my fair share over a long career, and I will tell you about a few of those later on. The key was to learn from each experience, absorb the lesson, and make it a stepping-stone to becoming a better pilot.

Over time, I realized that every day, every flight, is a learning opportunity. You learn from the good flights, and even more from the challenging ones. You learn from the people whom you admire, and also from those in whose footsteps you would rather not follow.

A good pilot never stops learning. Being a pilot is a lifetime journey, one that I embraced with all of my heart.

A Message for You

Be a selective sponge.
Learn learn learn.
Never stop.

CHAPTER 7

Every Dream Has its Price

S o here I was, a "real" pilot at last—a first officer flying a lovely big jet for a great airline. The dream had come true for that little Trinidadian girl who was told she could NEVER be a jet pilot. But every dream has its price—not only the price to get there, but the price to live there.

I'd been away from Trinidad for many years, during which I'd changed significantly because of living and studying abroad. My world view— my idea of what was right and possible—was now different from that of those I'd grown up with, those who'd watched me fly off to Canada and then gone on with their own lives.

When I returned home, everyone was delighted with my success and happiness because they cared about me. But I had broken the mold of what a Trinidadian female could do, and what she *should* do with her life. I no longer fit in.

First there was the social aspect. Being a female jet pilot in Trinidad in 1988 was not an asset to my dating life. I know; you'd think it would be a real plus, but it was the opposite. When I'd meet someone, the person would invariably ask, as people always do, *so, what do you do?* I soon learned that saying *I'm a pilot with BWIA* didn't serve me well. Their surprise was understandable, but I hated what always happened next. Our previously fun conversation would suddenly become awkward. The cute guy who'd been interested in me would turn pale and quickly drift away to another girl whose job and paycheck wouldn't challenge his.

So began what became a lifelong habit of saying *I work for BWIA*. Let people make what they wished of that! Some automatically assumed that I was a flight attendant, some assumed ground staff. No one ever guessed that I was in the cockpit, and I didn't tell them until they became a friend, or they found out from someone else, or ran into me in uniform at the airport.

Another reason I became more reserved about telling strangers my occupation was the crime situation in Trinidad, which has gotten steadily worse over the years. To "fly" under the radar as much as possible, and stay alive, felt safer. Imagine: after years of struggling to become an airline pilot, I was now hiding that fact to have a normal life in Trinidad!

The few local men who had the courage to pursue me were attracted by the ways in which I was different from other woman they'd known. They found me fascinating, adventurous, and exotic— at least, until they felt secure enough in our relationship to demand that I stop being all those things and behave like a "normal girl"—by which they meant a normal Trinidadian girl.

I remember being told by one chap, after having declined his numerous proposals, that no one would ever want to marry me because I didn't cook!

Another suitor said he really *did* want to marry me, but he wanted a wife who would be home every night when he got home from work. Hmmm . . .

I had news for both of those guys—I never wanted to get married. I decided this when I was eighteen, and up to that point, I'd seen no reason to change that plan.

Another issue was *availability* for a social or personal life, which was a challenge for every single crew-member, whether pilot or flight attendant. Constant absence could put great stress on budding relationships, as well as established ones. Working for the airlines almost guarantees you'll miss a lot of birthdays, Christmases, and other special occasions. Unless you're high on the seniority list, odds are you'll spend the most important holidays in a hotel thousands of miles from your loved ones with only a TV and takeout food for company, which can be very lonely.

Imagine having a family of your own, as many crew-members do. Think of dealing with your child's illness from 4000 miles away, or missing your baby's first steps.

Anyone who flies for a living understands that these sacrifices come with the job. There's no denying that being away from home so much can be hard, sometimes worrying, and you will miss out on many important life moments. Your partner or your support system is all-important. You rely on them to keep the home fires strong and healthy and to take care of everything in your absence.

Add to that the all-important issue of sleep—or rather, the lack of it. As the aviation industry became more competitive, airline schedules became more demanding. Over the years, it became normal for crew-members to have several night flights each week. Imagine coming home from a red-eye, exhausted to the core. Your family haven't seen you for days, and they're longing to spend time with you. Your partner has been holding things together beautifully and looking forward to sharing news or family duties now that you're back. But all you want, after the initial hugs, is to find a dark quiet room and sleep.

As you can see, flying can be challenging to relationships!

After years of testing, I came up with some key requirements for a good partner for a lady pilot. Applicants should have a strong sense of self and enough confidence to be unthreatened by her strength or her job, no matter what their own profession might be. Insecure? Don't bother to apply. Jealous? Ditto. This is a career where your partner may spend half the time away from home. Trust (and trustworthiness) is essential on both sides. Add patience, tolerance, tenderness, and a huge compassionate heart. Bonus points if you like to cook!

When I found him, I married him. But that's another story.

A Message for You

If you love roses, you won't let their thorns scare you away.
Every dream has its price;
if you are following your heart, the price is worth it.

CHAPTER 8

Another Empty Kitchen

People often ask me what it was like being a female in a man's world. In those days, a woman in the cockpit was still a rarity, and in my culture it was considered an extraordinary situation. They wonder . . .

How did the male pilots handle having a woman in the cockpit?
Were any of them hostile, discriminatory, resentful?
How did it feel to sit so close beside a masterful male captain for so many hours, stay in the same hotel, and then fly back? All that proximity and conversation . . . surely something happened?

I have news for them:

To me, flying with a man by my side felt perfectly normal, beginning with my years at LIAT and continuing for many years at BWIA.

This situation was all I knew! I never flew with another female until 2000, when I became a captain myself. So being locked into a small cockpit with a man for hours, day after day, week after week, was natural and comfortable for me.

But being locked into a small cockpit with me wasn't so natural and comfortable for my captains—at least, not at the beginning. The first time I met a captain in the crew room, I often sensed his caution, a touch of wariness. I could tell he was wondering (as all the pilots did) *what's it going to be like flying with a girl?*

On our northbound flight, that caution would linger. I would feel my captain's uncertainty about how to speak to me—whether or not he could talk and joke with me like "one of the boys." I could feel him tense (just a little) as he prepared to land, wanting to impress me, perhaps thinking that if the landing was not perfectly smooth, he would be embarrassed in front of a girl. My presence definitely changed the comfortable male dynamics of the cockpit.

On the return flight southbound, everything was different. By then, the captain had relaxed with me, having realized that I was just another pilot trying to do my best and willing to learn and laugh at my silly errors, and even at theirs. From then on, I could add another captain to my list of mentors.

That was the story 99.9% of the time. However, one memorable captain thought that having a female in the cockpit was the worst possible idea in the world. I'll call him my "Another Empty Kitchen" captain.

Famous for his temper and misogynistic behavior toward females, I was nervous as I checked in for my first flight with him. He was known for showing scant respect for those he considered subordinate to him, and he treated the flight attendants like his personal servants, calling them "trolley-dollies." Get the picture?

Our flight from Trinidad to Jamaica had three landings, and for the entire journey we had someone, a male airline employee, sitting behind us in the cockpit jump-seat. With a male audience to play to, my captain immediately set the tone for our flight by telling the jump-seat passenger that my presence in the cockpit meant "another empty kitchen." This comment was *not* said in jest, and it signaled the beginning of his harassment campaign.

After my landing in Barbados, I was delighted when the jump-seat passenger complimented me, and then horribly embarrassed as my captain proceeded to loudly criticize my technique and skills in support of his "another empty kitchen" theory.

My captain continued his obnoxious behavior toward me and the flight attendants and I felt ashamed and powerless. By our second stop in Antigua, I was almost seething—and I do not rise to anger easily.

By the time we landed in Jamaica, I was furious. I wondered how I could possibly maintain professional calm and equanimity on the next day's return flight. I dreaded that southbound flight with all my heart.

The next day, a different male passenger sat in the jump-seat all the way home. *A new audience for my captain to play to.* True to form, he didn't miss the opportunity to show off, insult me, and be chauvinistic to every female who entered the cockpit. His behavior was mortifying. I held tightly to the checklists and uttered not a word more than what was required by my job.

When we landed in Trinidad, the passenger departed, and the captain reached back and pulled the cockpit door shut. He then proceeded to tear apart my flying skills, my operating practices, my entire performance as his first officer.

I sat, trembling between dismay and outrage, saying nothing. In those days, in the cockpit the captain was king, the commander of the airplane.

Should I say nothing, just be humble and polite, and keep my job? Or should I stand up to him, in which case he could report me? My future career could be endangered, I might be victimized for making trouble . . .

Those thoughts flashed across my mind as he continued ranting. When he was through, he probably expected me to humbly apologize. I couldn't do it.

"Captain, I also need to talk."

He stared at me in surprise. Then he grunted, which I took as assent. I threw it all on the line—caution, my career—I didn't care.

I told him exactly what I thought of his behavior, his attitude, his lack of professionalism for the last two days. I asserted that I had done my duties to a high standard, that I knew I was a good pilot, and that he refused to see it because of his personal bias. I told him everyone feared him and disliked his behavior, and that he would get a lot more out of his team if he treated them like human beings.

He listened without saying a word. I stopped and waited, bracing for what would come next. "I apologize," he said. I was stunned. We shook hands silently and left the airplane.

He never reported me. I never reported him. I didn't know what to expect the next time we flew together, and I was apprehensive. To my surprise, on our next flight he was like a big gentle bear, treating me with care.

From that moment, things were different between us. His behavior did not significantly improve with anyone else, but he was always respectful toward me. He even shared some of his favorite tips and techniques. One day, I heard on the pilot grapevine that in reference to me he actually told someone, "There are only a few women in BWIA for whom I have any respect, and she's one of them."

I actually thank this captain for what he taught me—not only for the flying tidbits, but also for some useful life lessons, all of which helped make me the pilot I became:

> Never hesitate to speak my truth and stand up to bullying.

Knowledge and experience do not necessarily make a great captain.

A great captain should also be a good people manager, a true leader of the team.

I learned what not to model. I realized what kind of captain I did *not* want to become. I would walk another path.

And you know what?
If my being a pilot meant there was another empty kitchen, I was fine with that.

A Message for You

When it matters, stand up and be counted.

CHAPTER 9

_____

Learning from the Scary Stuff

"Did you have any *scary* experiences as a pilot?" It's another favourite question.

Sure. Many situations tested my courage, which is inevitable over a flying career as long as mine. But obviously (since I'm here talking with you), none were disastrous thanks to all the stringent procedures, training, and standards that are in place with any good commercial airline to assure safety as a top priority.

But at some point in every pilot's career things will go wrong, no matter how careful we are. The good news is that we are always on the alert for what might go wrong, and we are trained to handle the situation when things *do* go wrong.

This is where regular simulator training comes in—and BWIA's simulator training program was known to be among the best. To describe the sessions as intense would be like calling a tiger a pussycat. In order to ensure that pilots are ready and able to handle almost any challenges they might face in the air, everything that could go wrong with an airplane was re-enacted in the simulator.

The two pilots being "checked" (a polite word for putting us through our worst airplane nightmares) were expected to work as a team, handling multiple emergencies while flying calmly and competently through bad weather, then making a perfect landing with one engine, no hydraulics, and heaven knows what else.

We could hear the training captain chuckling behind us as together we struggled to fly a crippled airplane, go through multiple checklists, brief imaginary flight attendants and passengers, navigate through terrible weather, and somehow get us all safely on the ground—or, occasionally, into the imaginary sea.

The simulator was usually freezing cold, yet both of us would be pouring sweat and my curly hair standing on end. The simulator represented something of a love-hate relationship: I hated the stress, but I loved the adventure and the sense of accomplishment. After surviving sim, I felt I could handle anything! Well, almost anything . . .

In fact, the simulator sessions did their job beautifully. The rigorous training gave us confidence and skill and helped us work together smoothly to handle challenges.

When, over the course of my career, I did experience scary situations (the odd hydraulic failure, engine shutdown, cracked windshield) these events were no longer scary because both pilots in the cockpit had seen them before; we knew what to do, and we knew what the airplane was capable of. In fact (and I probably shouldn't tell you this), it was a thrill to be able to use our skills and expertise in a real situation. Such a crisis was what we had trained for, and we were ready! Excited—that's how I felt.

Even so, I will never forget one scary event that played a huge part in determining the kind of pilot, the kind of captain, I would become.

My first year of winter operations, I was a new first officer flying the MD83 jet. I had never had to deal with ice and snow on an airplane because, during my years as a flight instructor in Toronto, our little Cessna airplanes were not equipped with anti-icing equipment, so we stayed clear of icing conditions.

I had read all the manuals, and I had trained in the simulator, so my head was full of theory, facts, numbers. I thought I was ready for icing conditions, but I had no experience. That was about to change, big-time.

A few days before Christmas, Toronto experienced a huge blizzard. Passengers had been stranded at the snowbound airport for a couple of days, and now that the storm seemed to be easing, snowplows were clearing the runways. Departure looked possible if the weather continued to improve, so we set about the pre-flight.

That's when I realized, from the information in our de-icing manuals, that conditions were still too extreme for us to depart. I approached my captain, an experienced and respected senior pilot, and presented my calculations.

He rejected them.

Years later, as a captain myself, I understood why.

The captain represents the interests of the company, the passengers, the airplane. That day, my captain had to consider many things: the weather, safety, the angst of the stranded passengers, the desire of our Flight Operations Department to get the airplane back to Trinidad, since it had been stuck in Toronto for days. Everything.

My captain must surely have felt the huge pressure, as all eyes turned to him for a decision.

Besides, the storm *was* easing, and on the radio we could hear a couple of other aircraft preparing to depart.

He decided to go. Now.

I tried to explain again, to go through the numbers so he would see. He was offended, and I was rebuffed. I didn't know what to do.

Those were the old, old days of aviation, when the captain was literally the commander of the airplane, and his word was considered law. And I? Who was I? A new first officer with no real-time experience in this type of situation.

At that point, I had a choice:

> Politely decline to proceed, and walk off the airplane. The flight would be cancelled, and I would have to face the repercussions. My budding career would probably be over before it had begun.

> Or shut the heck up, trust in the experience and wisdom of my captain, sit down and do my job.

I chose to stay.
That decision changed my life forever.

There followed the most challenging takeoff I ever experienced in all my years of flying. When we were finally out of the storm and flying in clearer skies, my captain turned to me.
"Wendy, I am sorry. I should have listened to you."

I appreciated his apology but took no pleasure in receiving it. You see, I was also to blame, because I failed to stand up and be counted.

That day, two lessons were seared into my memory forever:

> I resolved this would never, EVER happen again. I would find the courage to do what I knew was right—regardless of the consequences.

> I learned that the captain is not infallible. We are all human, and humans can make mistakes. That's why there are two of us in the cockpit. We are supposed to be a highly functioning team. Together we are stronger!

This scary incident defined the kind of captain I wanted to become—and hopefully, I did become.

A Message for You:

You can learn from the scary stuff.
With preparation and training, the scary stuff can be handled.
The more you face your challenges, the easier they become—
and the more confident You become.

PART TWO

EAGLE
1999-2014

The whole power of the universe is living and breathing in you.

CHAPTER 10

Captain Wendy

O
n my first flight as a captain, I walked through the airport feeling like a complete fraud. In spite of the four brand new shining bars on my shoulders, I wondered if anyone could see I was a rookie, that this was my first day on the job.

I boarded the fifty-seat Dash 8 that was now under my command. I sat in the left seat, unaccompanied by a check-pilot for the first time. The moment of truth had arrived. All eyes were upon me, and the choice was mine: Be the captain, or go home. Of course, going home was not an option. I took a deep breath, dove into my new role, and never looked back.

That was in 1999, after being a BWIA first officer for eleven years.

Being a captain was a whole new experience in ways I never expected. First, I had not really considered what being the first *female* captain would feel like. The milestone was indeed an important one for women and for our country, and in recognition of its significance I initially agreed to the media publicity the airline requested. I quickly realized, however, that I was not comfortable with all the attention, so, after a few weeks, I opted out of the spotlight. For the rest of my career, I kept a low profile except for school appearances and small but meaningful projects.

When I was a first officer, I looked to the captain sitting in the left seat for guidance. Now *I* was the person in that left seat, and the first officers were turning to me. This change took a while to get used to. They expected me to hold the answer to their questions, to make the final decision. The buck stopped with me, in that left seat. Even so, whenever things got tough in the years ahead, I still looked to my left— out the window, into the sky, because God was sitting in *that* seat.

Oh, there was so much to learn! I learned that a first officer sees only a slice of the pie (if you consider all the aspects that make a successful flight like a pie). The captain is expected to see the entire pie, all 360 degrees of it, so I strove to see more of the pie. I spent the rest of my career trying, and along the way it dawned on me that the captain can't possibly see the entire 360 degrees without using the skills of the surrounding team.

I learned that no man is an island and that the entire team is crucial. A good captain works together with his/her team, empowering them, listening to them, and inspiring them. Since I wanted to become a *great* captain, this was my goal on every flight.

Over the next three years as captain on the Dash-8, I became comfortable being in the command position. My shoulders grew figuratively stronger and broader, my confidence deepened, my understanding of what it took to be a worthy captain grew with every flight. Then, late in 2000, I had the pleasure of flying with a female first officer for the first time, making history as BWIA's first all-female crew.

In 2002, I moved onto the new B737-800 as a first officer to become fully acquainted with the airplane before moving into the left seat as captain almost two years later, in 2004. When that time came, I felt like I had always belonged in the left seat of a B737. I was home!

So many memorable moments lay ahead. Of special significance was BWIA's first all-female jet flight to New York in 2005 where every single crew-member on board, both in the cockpit and the cabin, was a woman. Over the years, all-female cockpits happened often, never failing to create a frisson of excitement among the passengers, whether they were thrilled or terrified. Just as special were the occasions when I was the only woman on the crew. This little lady captain walking through an airport with five large males following her always created quite a stir.

When people see the pilot's uniform, they often assume that the person wearing it is lucky and privileged. I surely felt lucky and indeed privileged that I got the chance to live my dream, but succeeding was not easy, nor was the life easy. No outsider understands the demands of a life in the skies: the many challenges of the job, the wear and tear on the body, the difficulty of having a normal social and personal life, to name just a few. You cannot judge the journey by those glittery stripes on a snazzy uniform. Pilots work hard to get where they are, and they pay a steep price to stay there.

But 1 truly loved my career.
Even after so many years, flying an airplane thrilled me, especially the speed and power of the jets. I loved thundering down a runway into the sunrise; I delighted in flying at 37,000 feet over the sparkling lights of a sleeping city. I valued the opportunities—no, the demands—this job presented to keep learning, growing, trying to exce!. I enjoyed helping my first officers to become future great captains. I loved working as a team with my crew. I went home filled with pride and satisfaction when we all had a perfect flight.

Being a captain felt wonderful to me—not for the power of command, but for the ability to make a difference. I compare being the PIC (pilot in command) of a flight to being the conductor of an orchestra. Many people are involved, each with a vital part to play, and your part is to pull it all together, to draw the best out of every person. You manage the timing, tweak this and that, keep an eye on the whole picture; and when it all comes together just right, the result is the beautiful symphony of a great flight.

In spite of many challenges over the years, when anyone asks about my flying career, the word "magical" features somewhere in my response. Now how many people get to say that?

A Message for You

Follow your Dream.
Yes, You Can

CHAPTER 11

Other People's Opinions

"Excuse me. Are you a little boy or a little girl?"

The tiny old lady was blocking my path through the airport and looking me up and down. I was on my way to Toronto and in full captain's regalia: hat, jacket, flight bag. I stopped and looked down at her. "I beg your pardon, ma'am?"

"Are you a little boy or a little girl?"

This was a first for me. "Could you please explain?"

"Well," she said, "I see your pilot's uniform, so you must be a little boy. But you're wearing lipstick and heels!"

For a moment I was taken aback, but then I got it. There I was, striding boldly across the airport, assuming that anyone could see that I was indeed a pilot (from my uniform) and a female (hair, heels and lipstick). To me, my female pilot status was self-evident. I had forgotten that, for some people, the idea of a girl becoming a pilot was inconceivable. This little old lady's generation could never imagine a pilot looking like me. In her worldview, which comprised all she had ever known:

> Pilots were male.
> Girls couldn't fly airplanes.
> Boys don't wear lipstick and heels.

That made her question perfectly sensible. Her eyes were telling her what her brain could never compute. I was disturbing her gender programming. I give her credit for coming right up to me and asking me. How many people over the years had just watched me and wondered? I smiled, saying gently, "Ma'am, I am a little girl," and continued on my way.

My becoming a captain in 1999 was a big deal in my country, a local version of the first lunar landing. Who would have thought it could actually happen? The event definitely symbolized one small step forward for Trinidadian women! Almost overnight, I was viewed as a role model for local women and girls.

Still, it's hard to change generations of ingrained beliefs. This new phenomenon (a woman in charge of an airplane!) would take years to be generally accepted.

In the beginning, many passengers displayed shock, nervousness, and doubt. One man actually panicked when he heard my voice on the PA system and started to hyperventilate. We had to return to the gate and let him disembark. He took another flight.

I was saddened when I realized that the male passengers were not the only ones troubled by my presence in the cockpit. Many women were uncomfortable, sometimes terrified, when they realized I was in command of their flight. Time and time again, I reminded myself that they were just reflecting their own upbringing, every message that they had been taught. In their belief system, ladies didn't fly airplanes and could never be good at flying planes—and here they were, in the hands of a female captain. Surely, their lives must surely be in danger!

Over time, people's acceptance of women in non-traditional positions grew, and "oh-oh" changed to *"Wow"* . . . with both males and females sending congratulatory notes to the cockpit or insisting on shaking my hand when leaving the airplane. Upon seeing my mass of curly hair, one delighted dreadlocked Jamaican yelled, "The lady captain is a Rasta! We good, yes!"

To see all those excited faces was a delight, especially the young women and girls. My presence in the cockpit, particularly in the captain's seat, confirmed that their dreams were possible. Times were indeed a-changing!

And what did my co-workers think of flying with a lady captain? I believe the flight attendants were proud of their Captain Wendy, possibly because I was originally one of them (BWIA flight attendant 1973-1976). To be 100% sure, you should probably ask them yourself, but here is what I overheard through the cockpit door:

> Flight attendant (*the special PA announcement, spoken proudly and clearly with emphasis*):
>
> > "Captain **WENDY** Yawching is in command of our flight today, and **SHE** has given us a flying time of . . .
>
> Boarding passenger (*hesitantly*): "Is that a woman pilot I see in the cockpit?"
>
> Flight attendant (*warmly*):   "Yes, sir—and she's one of the *best*!"

I am forever grateful for their support and many kindnesses.

The engineers, I believe, respected me. A rumor was flying about that Captain Yawching knew her stuff, which sometimes led to interesting discussions about airplane issues.

And my fellow pilots? I will never know for sure, but I believe I was generally liked as well as respected for my passion and excellence. I also suspect some people found me to be a bit of a pain *because* of my passion for excellence.

At first, some of the younger first officers were nervous about flying with me because they had heard of my high standards. Over time, they became my biggest fans because, like the captains who had taken me under their wing all those years ago, I did my best to share the wisdom of my experience and to empower them to stretch and grow.

All of this is what I surmise; the truth is, I'll never know for sure what people thought of me. In fact, none of us will ever know for sure what the world thinks of us.

It doesn't matter. What *does* matter, for each of us, is this:

> Aim to be your best, most amazing self, no matter what you choose to do with your life.
>
> Accept that whenever you choose to do something outside the norm, people will stare, wonder, talk, and often criticize.
>
> Walk gently through the noise; stay focused; and do what you were meant to do to the very highest level you can.
>
> Follow your Star.

A Message for You

Listen to the voice within, not the noise outside.

CHAPTER 12

Captain Wendy's Mum

W hen I became a BWIA pilot and later a captain, my family was proud of me. My brother and sister found ways to let me know my job was pretty cool, as long as I didn't let it go to my head. My dad always supported whatever his children wanted to do with their lives and was simply delighted. His greatest wish was that his children be happy.

But my mum? She was my biggest fan.

This may sound like a foregone conclusion—isn't that what mothers do, support their children?— but it's not; Mum's support was a long time coming.

You see, my mum never wanted her daughter to become a pilot.

When I was young, her lack of enthusiasm was because . . . you got it: girls don't fly airplanes. In her mind, her daughter becoming a pilot was out of the question, *impossible*. She wanted me to forget that crazy idea and use my God-given brain to get a degree, a good job (by which she meant secure and conventionally professional), and, of course, get married and have kids. Perfect.

At age twenty-one, when my first serious suitor proposed, my mother was thrilled. He was everything she wanted for her daughter: tall, reasonably attractive, successful, and financially secure enough so I would not have to work unless I chose. He loved me to distraction and wanted to give me the world. Mum was distressed when I said no. What was I waiting for? Wasn't this every girl's dream?

She forgave me when I left to study in Canada (he didn't) because, in her mind, a university degree meant financial security for her daughter no matter what happened "down the line."

You see, when my parents' marriage splintered and broke, Mum found herself struggling to raise three hungry teenagers on alimony payments. With only a high school education and no work experience, her job options were limited. Those were lean years, and from those years came her resolve that her daughters would never struggle as she had, that we would never be dependent financially on a man, as she had been—although she still believed in marriage and wanted that for all of us.

When I got my degree in mathematics and computer science, Mum happily breathed a huge sigh of relief. I was poised to become financially independent, safe, and secure. She thought she could stop worrying now.

However, when I decided to pursue my childhood dream of becoming a pilot, she sighed again. What on earth was wrong with me? I could come back home and get that great IT job and (that pre-requisite to happiness!) get married. What was I thinking! Besides, airplanes were dangerous. She began to worry again.

When I got my first job as a pilot at LIAT in 1986, her resistance started to melt. Maybe that's when she finally realized I was serious about flying and deliberately walking away from the safe, secure future she imagined for me. Mum loved her children madly, and could see that I was over-the-moon happy. Yes, I suspect that's when she began to accept my choice.

Optimistically, however, she still hoped that one of those nice handsome LIAT pilots would catch my eye, and I might get married in Antigua and have a couple of babies. Perfect.

When I returned to Trinidad in 1988 to fly for BWIA, she was ecstatic. By this time she was comfortable with the idea of my flying and had begun to accept my assurances that airplanes were statistically safer than automobiles. She was happy that I was happy, even though I still hadn't married. She began to tell people, even relative strangers: "My daughter is a pilot." She was proud of the unconventionality of it, of her daughter's having the courage to fly!

When I became the first lady captain, she seriously lost it—which brings me to the story of *The Orange Flag*.

For my first three years as a captain, I flew the fifty-seater Dash 8 turboprop that serviced the smaller islands, Caracas, and Guyana. By then, Mum had retired to Tobago. On every Tobago flight, I would call her just before we departed and ask air traffic control for approval to make a left turn after take-off instead of the customary right turn. This left turn enabled us to fly roughly over my Mum's property.

After takeoff, the plan was to fly straight head towards the Magdalena complex, then turn left and fly north for about a minute, then make another left turn and set course to Trinidad. Keep an eye out for Mum's green roof surrounded by tons of purple bougainvillea—and the orange flag. My normally reserved, elegant, dignified mum would be outside on her veranda, frantically waving a huge orange banner. I never knew where she got that thing, but it was BIG and impossible to miss, especially against a background of green and purple.

At first, my co-pilots could not believe it. Captain Wendy's mum was clearly a little nuts! Then it became a matter of pride, skill, and fun for my first officers to fly right over that madly waving bright orange flag before turning left and heading for home.

What's the Message of this Story?

If someone loves you, even if they disagree with your choices, they will eventually come round when they see that you are happy and fulfilled. When you succeed, they will be proud of you and happy for you. So have faith that if you follow your dreams, one day your skeptics will transform into your greatest fans. Your job is to stay on course, show them all that you were meant for this and you mean business. Those who truly love you will eventually come around. Those who don't? Gently let them go . . .

CHAPTER 13

A Day in the Life - Part 1

T he scariest part about being a pilot in Trinidad had nothing to do with flying an airplane. The scariest part had to do with crime.

In those years, the crime situation in Trinidad grew from surprising (for a little Caribbean island) to shocking. The root causes are too many and complex for this kind of book. But the fact remains that in that beautiful, multi-dimensional tropical island, the scourge of crime was real, tangible, terrifying.

To be seen as someone with wealth or prestige (and pilots were believed to have both) was dangerous. You risked being targeted, robbed, kidnapped, even killed, and your family was also at risk. Pilots and their families were prime targets, especially since we were often away from home, leaving our families vulnerable. Primarily for this reason, I decided early on to keep a low profile about being a BWIA pilot.

I know of fellow pilots who were held up at gunpoint and their families terrorized. Flight attendants' cars were pursued down the highway with bandits shooting at them. Life in Trinidad at that time was like living in the Wild Wild West, and I resolved to do everything I could to stay safe.

In those days, I lived alone. My flight schedule included a hefty proportion of night flights, so I was often on the road heading to or from the airport in the wee hours when most people were fast asleep—except for the bandits.

I'd like to share my typical routine for a nighttime departure. Let's say the flight departs at 4 a.m.

7:00 p.m. Go to bed to ensure proper rest for the flight ahead.

1:00 a.m. When the alarm sounds, prepare for departure, keeping the lights off so anyone who might be watching "the lady pilot's house" won't realize I'm on the move. The streetlight outside provides enough illumination for breakfast, showering, and dressing—but not for the lipstick. I'll do that at the airport.

I put on my basic uniform (black pants, white shirt), leaving off any identifying emblem: no epaulettes or wings. My pilot's hat is already in the car. I pull a light sweater over the white shirt to make it less . . . white.

2:00 a.m. Get ready to leave home.
(I stowed my packed travel bags into the car last night so I can make a speedy departure this morning.)

Standing at the door, my keys in hand for doors and vehicle, I scan the outside for movement of any kind. Nothing. Swiftly, I open both the main door and the metal grill gate. I'm at a moment of maximum exposure as I turn around—fully visible under the bright security light—and lock both house doors, then click open the car, and jump in, immediately locking the car doors, breathing quickly. So far, so good.

I start the car and reverse into the street, so very vulnerable as I turn out and position to drive down the dark road. I peer into the blackness, aware that every bush or shrub could hide a bad man, that any shadow might jump out and shoot.

The moment I'm clear, I accelerate, surge away, my car

always in top condition, ready for a speedy departure and possible car chase.

(Once I did have a scary car chase at night, but that's for another story.)

I breathe normally again—*I made it!*—but I'm still alert, watching behind for possible followers. Now for the forty-minute drive to the airport.

Both route choices lead me through a no-man's land where, in the event of a flat tire or system failure, I will be a tasty morsel for any human vultures that happen by: a little female pilot all alone stranded in her car on the highway in the dark night.
That scenario doesn't bear thinking about.

In case you think that I am over-dramatizing, let me tell you about an incident I experienced myself:

One rainy, misty morning, I was making this same run to the airport. Because of the conditions, I was driving more slowly than normal, which saved me from running at speed over the logs that had been placed in the middle of the highway by bandits to derail vehicles so they would crash and their occupants become prey. My slower-than-normal speed and pilot's reflexes allowed me to maneuver around the series of logs. As they blurred by, I spotted the group of men clustered on the side of the highway, waiting . . .

This experience was the reality. Other times, bandits strewed nails on the asphalt and waited for the resulting flat tire stop.

So believe this: *I am not exaggerating the danger.*

The miracle is that in all those years, so few of us didn't get trapped—and that I, so very vulnerable as a female pilot—never got trapped at all.

On arriving at the airport, I breathe a sigh of relief. In the carpark, I put on my lipstick, bars (epaulettes) and hat, and emerge—head high and beautiful—to enter the airport as a BWIA pilot.

2:45 a.m. Check in.

Now for the part I love to do, the part I live to do: It's time to *fly*.

Why am I Telling this Story?

I'm telling this story because people don't know this story—
because they see the glamour, the perks, the travel,
but they never see the dark underbelly.
How could they? No one talks about it.
I am sharing this window into my world so you can understand:

. . . Just how much I loved being a pilot.

. . . That you should never envy the achievements of others
since you don't know what their journey has been.
You have no idea what they have given up to get there—
or what challenges they face even as they live their dream.

. . . That sometimes, doing what you love can be rough,
challenging, and even scary.
But if you love it, you'll never be fulfilled
unless you stay on course and do it anyway.

I'm so glad I did!

CHAPTER 14

A Day in the Life - Part 2

S ome things never change.

Each time I enter the cockpit, stow my flight bag, and clamber into that pilot seat is like coming home. I look around and above, at the glowing instruments and the lights, buttons, levers and circuit breakers, and I can't wait to get my hands on them. I am happy, excited, primed.

I begin my part of the pre-flight checks. Across from me, the first officer does his/her part, each of us intent on performing our piece of the whole. It's a partnership in which we have different moves that somehow mesh together to create a complete dance.

Passengers begin boarding. The load sheet arrives. The baggage holds
are closed, and we are ready for an on-time departure. It's time to go
flying. We call ground control for clearance to push and start.

When I was a young pilot flying smaller airplanes, I equated being
pushed back from the gate as the mark of being in the big league--and
now, here I am:

Captain Wendy: "Cockpit to ground"
                 "Go ahead Skipper"
                 (*comes the voice from the headset below*)

Captain Wendy: "We've been cleared to push and start.
                 Brakes are released."

The tow truck below eases us away from the gate with care,
watchful eyes on the ground ensuring we are clear of any hard
objects from wingtip to wingtip, from nose to tail.

"Captain, you are clear to start engines number two and one."

The first officer and I run through the checklist to start the engines. Both
start as smooth as silk. We can't really hear the engines in the cockpit,
only a gentle thrum, but the cockpit instruments tell us all is well. Outside
is a different story: those twin jet engines are roaring so loudly the ground
crew need protective gear. We do another checklist after starting the
engines, then get clearance to proceed to the active runway.

A pilot's day is full of checklists. We will call for them (pilot speak for
requesting that a particular checklist be read) and do them together, at
every stage of the flight ahead. Before takeoff, after takeoff, at cruise,
before descent, before landing, after landing, and again after shutting
down the engines at destination. We have checklists for normal
operations, and we also have a special collection of checklists for almost
anything that could go wrong with an aircraft.

Over the years, I've learned how vital these checklists are. When a
person is under pressure, it can be so easy to miss something crucial,

something that could make the difference between success and failure, life and the other option.

Air Traffic Control: "West Indian 426, taxi into position and hold."

Air Traffic Control clears us onto the active runway. Looking out carefully for anything that might spoil our day, we rumble onto the runway and line up with the white centerline. All checklists are complete, passengers and cabin crew briefed that departure is imminent. The moment everyone is waiting for has come.

Air Traffic Control: "West Indian 426, you are cleared for takeoff."

It's time to Fly.

Advance power levers.

The engine instruments wind up and are monitored; all is well.

Release the brakes . . . and the huge metal tube with 150 souls on board starts to roll forward, then hurtle forward.

I love this feeling of being pushed back into my seat by the surge of those powerful engines with the ribbon of runway stretching ahead of me, the sky beckoning beyond . . .

80 knots. All is well.

100 knots.

V1. The moment of decision:

If something happens before V1. speed, we can still stop safely on the runway.

If something happens after V1. speed, we are committed to take the aircraft into the air, no matter what the problem.

Vr. Takeoff speed. Slight pressure on the yoke, the nose eases up, the nose wheel leaves the ground, followed seconds later by the main gear.

This is the moment of transformation, of magic. This is the moment when a huge heavy airplane departs the earth and transforms into a beautiful graceful metallic bird.

This is what it was meant to do. This is what I was meant to do.

It's nighttime, five hours later, and we are 250 miles out of New York and our destination, JFK International Airport. Time to prepare for arrival. We check the weather, the runways in use, and conditions at our alternate airports in case for some reason we are unable to land at JFK. All look good so far. My first officer and I discuss everything as we review the approach charts, the specifics of the landing, and our plans if we need to proceed to another airport. The flight computers are programmed, descent checklist completed. We are ready.

ATC instructs us to begin descent from our cruising altitude. The descent is a step down process in terms of both altitude and speed. The closer we get to the high density airspace around JFK, the more crucial it is that we be alert, focused, responsive, and a highly functioning team.

We are being guided by ATC to fit into a three-dimensional jigsaw puzzle of huge metal parts, all moving at speed and potentially explosive. The focal point of that puzzle is JFK airport and the landing runways in use. Tonight two runways are in use, parallel to each other. Aircraft will be landing (and others taking off) simultaneously on both of these runways.

When the scattered clouds permit, we can see the lights of other jets above, below, ahead, and to each side of us, but we can't see the whole picture. Only the faceless voices commanding us from the ground can see the entire puzzle, and at this stage we must trust them with our lives, as our passengers have trusted us with their lives.

Our job is to strive to do everything perfectly as instructed and so avoid disrupting their tightly woven precision patterns. ATC is busy juggling balls of steel; they don't have time for non-compliant pilots.

ATC: "West Indian 426. Turn left heading 060. Reduce speed to 180 knots. Descend to 3000 feet."

We comply promptly. This is what we have trained for. The density of traffic and the instructions (and the pilot performance needed) become more and more intense as we are turned toward the active runway. We are slotted into an approach sequence between a B767 ahead and an Airbus 340 behind us. We are number two to land.

The B767 touches down and now we are number one.

ATC: "West Indian 426. Cleared to land."

Highly alert, flying the precision glide path to the landing zone . . . Touching down, reversers, brakes, vacate the runway as soon as possible to facilitate the Airbus coming in close behind us.

Now we are in the hands of ground control, who will talk us through the maze of taxiways to the terminal building. As we arrive at the international terminal, our ground marshallers are ready to guide us safely into our assigned gate.

Engines shut down.
Checklist complete.
Paperwork done.

We are here, another flight safely completed. I am tired, I am happy. I still can't believe I am paid to do something I love so much. Tomorrow we will do it all over again, heading home.

I hope you enjoyed this small peek into my world.

I pray you have, or will have, something in your life that you love as much;
something to which you give your heart, your hands, your head.
When that happens, it won't feel like work,
because you will be following your passion.
You will know that you are living the life you were meant to live.
Never settle for less.

CHAPTER 15

A Woman in a Man's World
An Interview with Captain Wendy

Q. What was it like, being a woman in a man's world?

A. I never considered the cockpit to be a man's world. It was a PILOT's world—and I was determined to be the best darned pilot I could be. That's it.

That determination defined my career, and, over time, I became known for my focus on excellence. As a first officer, that meant tucking my head down to lots of hard work and study and being eager to learn from the experiences and wisdom of my captains. My focus on excellence also involved pushing myself, challenging myself to do better every single time.

Q. Did you feel there was something to prove?

A. Not really, although it was clear that everyone was watching me, the first female in a flying position on BWIA's MD83 jets. My efforts to excel were for myself. It's just how I roll . . . I strive for excellence in any path I choose to follow. Seems to be my nature!

Q. Were you competitive?

A. Never. I actually believe that we can—and should—reach for the stars together. Everyone can be excellent if we help each other.

Q. Did the guys treat you any differently? Like . . . a girl?

A. That's an interesting question. Clearly I was a girl, but not like any that they had run into before. Remember, this was Trinidad, where the chemistry between men and women is celebrated, where in those days male machismo was the norm and BWIA pilots were no exception. Generally, the two sexes were considered different species, for good reason.
And now, here was Wendy.

At first, my captains approached me with caution. They weren't quite sure what to expect from a female in the cockpit:
Would I pull the girly card, and ask for help to do certain things?
Would I fold under pressure, e.g., scream in a thunderstorm?
Should they talk to me extra gently?
Should they flirt just a little?

Over time, they realized I was just another pilot, perhaps a little better looking than the norm. Also, because I was so passionate about flying and learning, over time my captains adopted me and tried to stuff me with all their own wisdom. Many are the captains I must thank for making me the pilot that I became. I am hugely grateful to them all.

Over time, my reputation grew. I heard rumors that a certain training captain would tell the pilots in simulator, "Wendy has no trouble with that, so what's your problem?"—which, of course, was not helpful to my popularity in the ranks. Engineers began to treat me with respect when they realized I understood some of the technical workings of the airplane well enough for a discussion. Everyone understood I would never shirk from doing whatever the job demanded, to a high standard . . . regardless of conditions. Like any other pilot, I would walk out into the dark, freezing, snowy Toronto night, all bundled up, to do the external pre-flight and climb onto the wings to check for ice.

No girly girl.

They could rely on me.

Q. Did you experience sexual harassment? Was it exciting to spend so many hours behind closed doors in a cockpit with a handsome man?

A. Other than the good natured joshing every Caribbean female grows up with and knows how to handle gracefully, no one ever "hit on" me in the cockpit, and I never experienced sexual harassment. You see, I don't think the male pilots thought of me as a "real girl," nor was I "one of the guys." I fell somewhere in between, like a cute mascot—and they treated me accordingly.

Q. You became a Captain in 1999. What's it like to be "a woman in a command position" in a man's world? How did YOU handle it? How did the guys handle it?

A. Everyone is understandably curious about this. Women were still a rarity in the cockpit in those days, and I had broken the "glass ceiling" in the cockpit when I became Trinidad and Tobago's first female captain. For sure, the eyes of the world were on me even more than before. People were wondering what kind of captain would I become, and how would I handle the new authority?

As is my nature, I was determined to become the best captain I could be.

Not female captain.

Captain.

Being a captain opened up a whole new world of learning and growing for me. My worldview expanded, as all of a sudden the buck stopped with me; the responsibility for a successful and safe flight rested on my shoulders. There was always something to learn that could help me to be a better captain. It was a lifetime of learning, growing, trying, improving . . . and helping others. As many captains had done for me years before, I took delight (and, I admit, great pride) in helping my first officers learn, grow, and challenge themselves. It was my turn to give back.

As for my fellow pilots, they handled this lady captain beautifully. I felt surrounded by respect. Always.

**What more can I share with you about
being a woman in a man's world?**

*First, don't expect special privileges simply because you're a woman.
Do the job to the highest possible standard.
Don't look for discrimination or issues,
but if they turn up, handle them professionally.
When it's important, stand up and be counted.
Don't try to behave like a man. You're not.
Just be the wonderful professional that only you can be.
And always strive for excellence.
Always.
Not to prove anything.
But because it's just how you roll.*

CHAPTER 16

The Shadows Within

Y ou might think from listening to my story so far that I was
always fired up and optimistic and confident and driven, that
I never had moments that turned me aside from my path and
filled me with doubt and fear.

Nothing could be farther from the truth.

Everyone goes through those periods, everyone has times when the
shadows within rise up and make them doubt themselves, afraid of the
future, afraid of taking risks or failing, afraid of changing their path,
of trying something new.

All my life, those feelings have been present. At times I wondered if
my dreams were crazy, fearing I would never measure up, feeling
the weight of all the forces arrayed against me: cultural norms, other

people's opinions, financial challenges, my age, my gender—so many limiting beliefs!

There have been many times when I just wanted to lie down and fold up my wings, when it was difficult to find the strength, courage, energy to get up and walk.

There have been times when, sick with pneumonia, I didn't have the energy to walk to the bathroom, and the thought that I could one day hike again, or dance again, was impossible to entertain.

There were times, heavy with loss of my Dad, or my husband, when I couldn't bear the thought of moving forward, when I was sinking into a grief so heavy that I felt I could never be happy again.

The thing is, I didn't let those moments define my life.

Whenever I am discouraged, sad, or afraid, I find refuge and healing in prayer, nature, and the support of my inner circle:

> Through prayer, I reconnect with the Divine. In this space, I become reacquainted with my highest self and the belief that I am an infinite being living in a human body, that I was given this gift of life for a reason, and that the fact I am still here means I have value, there is a purpose for my life.

> Through nature (especially being active in nature), I reconnect with the magic of Mother Earth and stock up on endorphins. It's hard to be stuck when you are moving, so sometimes, even when it's the last thing I feel like doing, I go outside and get my body moving and drink in the natural beauty all around me. Every single time, that stuck feeling, the heavy energy, shifts. If needed, I will do it again the next day, and the next . . .

> With the help of my friends and loved ones, I find support and hugs, a shoulder to cry on, an ear to hear my blues. I'm not good at listening to advice, but it helps me to talk and to feel that I am heard.

Everyone needs help sometimes. There is no shame in asking for it.

Along the way, I've made so many mistakes: I have chosen the wrong guys, made terrible financial decisions, said and done things I later regretted. I've spent many sleepless nights wondering if I was good enough, or if I should give up and reach for safer and steadier shores.

I know what it feels like to walk through a door, afraid of what's on the other side.
I know what it feels like to be so afraid that I couldn't step through the door without being pushed.

I have a picture of me crouched at the open door of a little airborne airplane in New Zealand, fully suited up for skydiving and attached to an instructor. I am holding onto the doorjamb, legs braced, looking down at the world 12,000 feet below, sheer terror on my face. This was the moment of truth: I was required to let go and roll forward into nothingness, trusting in my instructor to bring us both safely to earth. I simply could not do it.
I held fast to that jamb as if my life depended on it. As far as I was concerned, it did.

Realizing that I had lost my nerve, my instructor made the decision for me. It was time to go! He simply pushed us through the door. I was attached to his chest harness, so wherever he went, I went. As I tumbled out, rolling terrified into the sky, I was flooded with the absolute certainty that I was about to die—that we would both die.

And you know what? At that moment, I surrendered. If I was going to die, I may as well enjoy the ride until the big splat at the end. Seconds later, my instructor tapped my shoulder, the pre-arranged signal for me to spread my arms like an eagle. Since I had nothing to lose (I was going to die anyway), I spread my trembling wings.

At that moment, everything changed. I was a bird! I was flying!

In reality, I was plummeting downwards at terminal velocity attached to another human being. This free-fall was the most exhilarating thing

I had ever done. The wind rushed by, ripping at my clothing, roaring in my ears. The beautiful world turned slowly far beneath as my instructor maneuvered us toward the landing zone. I watched in wonder as the tiny fields and lakes, roads and houses, got bigger and bigger. All too soon, my instructor pulled the ripcord and the parachute opened. We floated gently to earth, sight-seeing.

The point is, that sixty second free-fall was the most amazing experience I had ever had; one I would never have known if I had not been pushed.

The next time I went tandem sky-diving (yes, there was a next time), even though I was scared, I had the courage to jump without being pushed. I knew what waited on the other side of that door, on the other side of that leap of faith.
Magic.

> ### A Message for You
>
> *Your fears or your dreams.*
> *You're going to have to let go of one of them!*
>
> —Gertrud de Witte

CHAPTER 17

Adventures Unlimited

Altitude sickness.
I'm at 13,000 feet above sea level, and I have altitude sickness—the deadly cerebral kind.

I wake up this morning in my tiny tent, but I cannot get up. Any attempt to raise my head brings excruciating pain. I have never had such a headache in my life. There is only one thing to do: Stay. Down.

Our expedition leader decides I will be fine as long as I do not proceed up the mountain, but the show must go on. He assigns one of the sherpas to be my support, and the rest of the group pushes on toward Everest Base Camp.

It's a crushing blow, since I had prepared for this trip for months and paid a lot of money to get here.

Altitude sickness was not totally unexpected, of course. I'd felt the headache building for days and watched two others from our group step aside as the fluid in their bodies leaked into the wrong places and laid them low.

Altitude sickness is a killer if you don't listen to its warnings. Just a few days earlier, we heard of a young athlete who pushed too far and died higher up the mountain. We watched the helicopter heading up to bring his body down.

The human body isn't designed to function well above 10,000 feet . . . because of atmospheric pressure. As you ascend, the pressure goes down, and the amount of oxygen you intake with each breath becomes lower. Lack of oxygen, however, is not what causes altitude sickness. The pressure itself is the problem—or, I should say, the differential pressure. As you ascend into thinner air, the pressure in your lungs may become lower than the pressure in your blood vessels, causing tiny blood vessels to leach blood into the lungs. The condition starts with a cough, then becomes worse as the fluid collects. You can literally drown in your own blood.

It's the same with your brain. Your blood pressure may cause tiny vessels to leach blood into the intercranial spaces of your skull, causing an incredible headache and, if left untreated, death.

Some people feel the effects of altitude at 8,000 feet, others are unscathed to 15,000 feet. Effects vary with physiology. No one can predict who will be affected at what altitude. My personal ceiling seems to be 13,000 feet.

So here I am, my worst fear confirmed. There is no doubt. I have to stop here.

Very sobering -	when a highly trained, fit body is suddenly helpless to move, even to sit up.
Very frustrating -	to say goodbye to my teammates, who are focused on achieving their goal of reaching the base camp at 17,598 feet above sea level.
Very disappointing -	After all the preparation, training, expense, and hard work to get here, was my Everest adventure over?

So I rest in my tent, giving my body what it needs: time to catch up, time to acclimatize.

By the next day, I can move gingerly, so I explore a little. It's a lovely place to be stranded, near to the famous Tengboche monastery. I can hear the bells, the chants of the monks inside. The mountain views are stunning.

Next day, I feel much better. Walking as much as I can, taking it slow and easy, I head down to lower altitudes then back up, to sleep at 13,000 feet, feeling stronger by the hour. My body is beginning to feel like it was born at this altitude, like my sherpa. This is why, on the third day, I propose that we press on up the mountain to see how far we can get before we meet our group coming down. My sweet sherpa nods in agreement with the crazy tourist lady, and so the next morning, we hustle down to the village below, hire a porter, and strike out for the beckoning heights.

I feel fit, strong and confident, powerful and fast. My body is now fully acclimatized. I pass other groups along the busy trail, with their members lying gasping on the rocks, doing exactly what we were doing just days before: walk thirty steps, then collapse to rest, panting; another thirty steps, pant some more. Not getting enough oxygen into your lungs, no matter how fit you are, will do that to you. I know! The next few days stand out as the most memorable of my entire

Himalayan adventure. No longer part of an "adventure expedition" group, I am instead traveling lean and fast with two locals, and everything is different.

Each day, I am welcomed into the tiny homes of their families, where they press me to eat and drink their simple mountain fare. Sitting on a dirt floor, I accept a steaming bowl of broth with chunks of potato from a pair of blackened hands with dirt-encrusted fingernails as a wizened face peers at me, wearing a million-dollar smile. Not a word understood between us. Priceless!

The days are fine and clear. Visibility is unlimited, the mountain peaks magnificent, the mighty Everest seeming so close as to be touchable. Temperature is 15 C (57 F) in the day, perfect for strenuous hiking. But it gets dark by 5 p.m. when the temperature plummets to -30 C (-22 F) within a few hours. The night is so cold that my water bottle (filled with boiling water and tucked into my sleeping bag) is frozen solid in the morning.

On the third day, as we prepare to make camp in the early evening, we can see Everest Base Camp in the distance. It's about 100 vertical feet above us but at least a five hour walk. Tomorrow, tomorrow! We've made it!
I have made it.

Then, out of the twilight, some familiar figures appear, my team, on their way down. They made it to base camp, but at a high price. One of the other females pushed herself too far and is on the verge of collapse. She cannot safely spend another night at altitude. They have to take her further down, now.

Will I come with them?
The decision is mine . . . continue on, reach my goal, the goal I worked so hard for, or— give it up, turn around now and head down with my team, the same team who left ME at the monastery.

I have always been goal-oriented. Like an arrow in flight, it's hard for me to change course in mid-air. I have never been a quitter.

I need to decide, *now*, because they must keep moving, down, down, to save her life . . .

I give it up.
I turn my back on the mountain, on the goal of Everest Base Camp.
I rejoin my team and help them support the ailing girl.
We camp lower down the mountain, and in a couple of days,
she fully recovers.

This decision was one of the harder decisions of my life.
I could have been the first Trinidadian to reach Everest Base Camp.
Instead, I was the first Trinidadian to *almost* reach Everest Base Camp.
I could have made it.
It was so close, it was just . . . over there, and I was fit and strong.

But I chose the team.

Looking back, I have no regrets (well, maybe a few small ones) because that decision taught me:
>I *could* turn the arrow in mid-flight.
>I could give up my own desires for a greater good.
>I didn't have to prove anything to anybody—once *I* knew what I was capable of.

A Message for You
Every moment is an opportunity to choose.

CHAPTER 18

Eco-Warrior

L iving in Canada had taught me to believe that I could do just about anything if I wanted it badly enough, put in the effort, and trusted in the Divine. That newfound belief system changed everything. No longer would I be defined by other people's ideas of what was possible. I would follow my heart.

My new sense of adventure led me to venture into the great Canadian wilderness where I became skilled at canoeing, camping, and hiking. I thought nothing of disappearing with a couple of friends into the wild for a week of pure nature, carrying a canoe on our heads across rocky trails, paddling as far from civilization as possible, to watch the stars, swim in icy, inky lakes, all the while keeping a keen eye out for bears and moose. In wintertime, even though I hated the cold, I pushed myself outdoors and learned to ski, discovering the breath-taking beauty of brilliant sunshine sparkling on snow-covered pine forests. My favorite ski-getaway was Whistler-Blackcombe in British Columbia, a place of staggering wintertime beauty.

By the time I moved to Antigua to fly for LIAT, the great outdoors had become a lifetime love affair. I started by exploring the many Caribbean isles. I hiked rainforests and to the tops of many an old volcanic peak. I learned to scuba dive in Dominica, which opened my awe-struck eyes to a whole new world: no longer was I looking down from above with a snorkel, now I felt like part of a beautiful underwater dance of incredible diversity.

When BWIA hired me in 1988, I continued my explorations, but now the entire world became my oyster. Over the years I have probably traveled half of the world in search of outdoor adventure. I've hiked the Rockies, Swiss Alps, the Southern Alps in New Zealand, to Machu Picchu in Peru—and, as you've heard, almost to the base camp of Mt. Everest.

In 1994 I took six months of no-pay leave from the airline and headed to the South Pacific. My plan was to travel around Fiji, New Zealand, Australia, Vanuatu, Tonga, and Samoa. Once again, my friends and family thought I was crazy, heading off alone to the other side of the world with just a backpack. I went anyway.

Those were the days when the Internet was a strange new concept. There were no emails, no Facebook, no IG moments, no WhatsApp. I had no cellphone. Most of the time, my family had no idea where I was or how I was until they received the postcards I had posted four weeks earlier. I had no idea what was happening at home because, by the time I got their news at a pre-arranged address, it was more than four weeks old. I was really on my own, and I loved it.

I lived cheaply, staying dorm-style in youth hostels and traveling by local bus and train. People were intrigued by this fuzzy-haired

Caribbean girl so far from home, and I made many "travel buddies," all exploring the world on a budget as I was.

The energy of Fiji reminded me of the Caribbean, even though the people spoke a different tongue and had very different customs. Fiji felt like home.

New Zealand was, and still is, one of the most beautiful outdoor countries I have explored. Here, I tried bungee jumping (once was enough, thank you) and did my first tandem parachute jump out of a perfectly good airplane (the joke goes that pilots never willingly jump out of a good airplane).

In Australia I met Aboriginal people, camped out under a million stars in the Outback, and scuba-dived the Great Barrier Reef.

In memorable Vanuatu, I stayed awhile in a hut made of mud and grass, where local children came to stare at me with shy smiles because, in their world, I was the strange one. I attended a sacred local ceremony in which men and boys, naked except for penis-sheaths, threw themselves headfirst off tall wooden towers. No, they didn't die, because the lianas that were attached to their ankles pulled them up just scant inches before their heads crashed into the ground. Below, their women-folk, wearing only grass skirts, danced and sang. The people observed this authentic annual ritual to assure a successful yam harvest. Afterward, I hiked to the top of an active volcano and stared down into its red, bubbling depths.

Tonga and Samoa were enchanting. The people were warm and delightful, and their cultures different from anything I'd experienced.

Over the course of this six-month journey, I was literally on the other side of the planet, as far from home as I could get. I learned what it felt like to be completely alone. I learned how precious my home relationships were, and also how to make friends anywhere in any language. With enthusiasm, I embraced new cultures, cuisines, and experiences. I saw how countries like New Zealand were determined to protect their environment and preserve their flora, fauna, and natural resources for future generations.

And I found a new calling.

You see, although I had long loved and enjoyed the natural gifts of our beautiful planet, on this trip I began to understand its fragility. I realized that we in the Caribbean were failing miserably by taking our natural bounty for granted in the unfounded assumption that Nature would take care of itself—that our land, our seas would always be beautiful and clean and bountiful, no matter what we threw at them.

I was inspired to make a difference.

I determined to do what I could to change the story.

I became an eco-warrior.

That's why, on my return home in 1995, I launched Wildways, Caribbean Adventure Travel. My vision was to convince the people of Trinidad and Tobago that there was value in protecting their beautiful natural resources. I had no idea how to do this, or how to run a business. What I had was passion, purpose, and the belief that I would be guided every step of the way.

At the time, eco-tourism was a new concept in Trinidad, practiced by only a few. The idea was that if locals realized foreigners would pay good money to hike in pristine rainforests or to see live leatherback turtles on a clean beach, they might be incentivized to protect them.

With my business partner, I also created an award-winning environmental awareness program for local secondary school children. Under our expert care and guidance, they were exposed for four weeks to the incredible natural wonders of their islands. Even though Wildways closed its doors in 2005, I consider that program to be one of the most meaningful ventures I've ever done.

A Message for You

*If we can change the way our children see the world,
our children can change the future.
If I can help you to change the way you see the world,
you can change your future.*

*You are not a one-dimensional being.
Don't choose to live a one-dimensional life.*

CHAPTER 19

Never Say Never

N ever.
Life has taught me this: Never say Never.

People told me that I could NEVER become a pilot. You saw how that turned out.

At age eighteen, I declared firmly to everyone in my life that I would NEVER get married. For thirty-two years, I stuck to that promise, breaking the hearts of several good men along the way. I had no problem with the idea of being in a committed monogamous relationship, sharing my life with someone I cared for, but—get married?

Never.

I didn't want to be tied down. I needed to know that I could leave, anytime. Most of the men I met were determined to make me into a version of their mother, or their concept of a perfect woman. I wanted to feel FREE, always, to be ME. Psychologists would likely say that my parents' broken marriage was at the root of it all.
Perhaps.

Whatever the reason, I was clear on this: marriage was not for me. I made it clear to the men who courted me: I will *never* get married. If this is a problem for you, then you've pursuing the wrong girl.

Over the years, my family and friends gave up on the idea of Wendy, married with kids. And then I met Erik.

The circumstances of our meeting were so unusual that I can only say *the universe brought us together*. That this relationship was something special was immediately clear to both of us.

Within a month, he asked me to marry him.
My reply? The normal one: I will NEVER get married.
Within another month, I said yes.
Why? Because Erik was clearly the man with whom I wanted to spend my life. Because I couldn't imagine being with another man, ever. Because he wanted to marry me with all his heart, and I wanted him to be happy more than I wanted to hold on to my old promise to myself.

So I said yes.
My family and friends were staggered.
Wendy is *what*? With a man that she met *when*? SIX months ago?
Yup.

We were married in an intimate ceremony on a lovely hilltop in Tobago, just six months after meeting, on my 50th birthday (yes, 50, not a typo).

By now you probably know that when I decide to do something, I do it wholeheartedly. I walked into marriage with Erik without the fears that had dogged my thoughts about marriage all those years. I was all in, fully convinced that this was what I was supposed to do next with my life.

So began a new journey, one in which I was no longer a Me. I was part of a WE. Wendy & Erik. We were two people who had lived full and rich lives and were fine alone, but better together.

My conjecture that being married might be the same as living together (which I had done a couple of times before) was soon blown out of the water. I discovered new depths of love, of commitment, of partnership.

Who would have ever thought it possible? Not me. Never.

One of the many blessings that Erik brought to our union was his unfailing enthusiasm and support for anything I wanted to do, to try, to learn. He never took away my sense of freedom; in fact, he supported it:

Flying? He was proud of his captain-wife.

Adventure trip? Let's do it!

Dance classes? Go ahead, honey. Have fun with your three dance partners, and when you come home, I'll be waiting with dinner ready. (Yes, he liked to cook.)

Oh—and did I mention he was a fabulous cook?

Our marriage didn't last forever, but many things don't. We had twelve, love-filled years together that were among the richest, most joyous, and most illuminating years of my life. I learned so much from that relationship, lessons that I couldn't have learned if I hadn't made the leap of faith with him. Those learnings were a necessary part of my own journey to becoming the person I am now and the foundation of the person I will become.

Why am I telling you this?

I'm hoping that my journey helps you to believe what I have learned:

It's OKAY to change your mind.
Don't be afraid to release that which no longer serves your greatest good.

It's OKAY to change your STORYLINE, no matter what your age.
In fact, the older you are, the more important it is to embrace change. One of the saddest things is to hear elders talk of the things they regret NOT doing with their lives.

It's YOUR life, YOUR journey, no one else's.
By having the courage to change your situation, your direction, you will develop in ways you never dreamed of. You'll discover new aspects of YOU that might never have seen the light otherwise. New doors will open, and new destinations will be possible.

To anyone who doubts your plans, say:
"I can. I will. Watch me."
Then go ahead and shock them.

A Message for You

Listen to your own heart.

I'm talking about the core of you,

that little quiet voice inside your center.

Your heart will never steer you wrong.

Listen, and then walk forward with faith and courage.

The gifts will be waiting for you, on the path with heart.

And . . .

Never Say Never.

CHAPTER 20

Lightning Does Strike Twice

Who says that lightning doesn't strike twice in the same place? They're wrong.

In 2017, I lost my beloved husband and my dad in the space of three weeks.

One was sudden and unexpected.
The other was expected and took a while, but was still a heartbreak.

It started with my husband.
One day in late June, a very difficult conversation with a terminal diagnosis . . .
Two weeks later, he was gone, never to be seen again.
He was the big love of my life. I was devastated as my world shattered into little pieces.

Three weeks later, my dad died. That second lightning strike was more gradual but searing nonetheless. Dad was ninety-three. He spent his last ailing months living in the studio of my home with his devoted second wife Kemlan by his side. Together, we walked with him to the very end. Even though we knew it was time for him to leave us, it was a huge blow when the actual moment came.

My grief was immeasurable. Within three weeks, I had lost the two most important men in my life, and I thought I would die of a broken heart. Still bleeding, I told my brother Dexter, "Please take care of yourself. I couldn't bear it if anything happened to you, too."

The thing is, it's rare to die of a broken heart, even though you may think you will. Then began one of the darkest periods of my life. Perhaps you have experienced this . . . ?

Each morning, waking up to black despair, feeling like I couldn't, simply couldn't face another day.

Dragging myself out of bed, finding the strength to start plodding, then walking, forward.

Heartbreak or not, certain things had to get done.

Day after day, doing the necessaries as best I could, and crying the rest of the time.

Friends and family could only do so much to help; the broken heart was mine.

Prayer helped hugely, of course, but wounds take time to heal, and grief has its own timetable.

It took me years to find my joy again.

That period of my life, the double-tap of heartbreak, reminded me of a BWIA flight when lightning actually did strike us twice:

I was still a first officer, flying southbound from New York to Antigua, then onwards to Trinidad. Thunderstorms surrounded the little island of Antigua. Strong gusty winds and wind shear on approach made it impossible for us to land safely. After two aborted attempts, the captain decided wisely (and per company procedure) to divert to Guadeloupe, only fifty-four miles away.

The weather in Guadeloupe was reported to be much better, but our way was blocked by a wall of thunderstorms from horizon to horizon. We didn't have enough fuel to go hundreds of miles to the left or right, and we couldn't go back to Antigua. We had to find a safe way though to Guadeloupe.

Everywhere, the radar showed red. Though the cockpit window, that red showed as huge black and green and yellow clouds. It was the first time I had seen green clouds! We picked our way gingerly through the storm when, without warning, a bolt of lightning came straight out of a black cloud ahead, aiming for the right side of the cockpit where I sat—

CRACKWHAM!

The plane jumped like God had lifted it up and dropped it. Screaming came from the cabin. If not for my seatbelt, I would have been on the captain's lap. I was terrified!

Within seconds, another bolt hit us exactly like the first; again, it seemed to be aiming for me. The plane lurched violently, accompanied by more screaming from the back. Then we were through the black-green wall. Clearer skies appeared ahead. Both pilots were shaken, unsure of what damage, if any, the aircraft had suffered by taking two direct strikes. We radioed ahead (surprised that the radios hadn't been sizzled) that we would need an engineer to check out the aircraft in Guadeloupe.

The only damage to the plane was two small, round, black holes in the wings where the lightning exited the aircraft. I was amazed at how resilient that aircraft was!

No one wants to get struck by lightning or a thunderbolt, but at some time in every life, out of nowhere a bolt will strike. No matter how strong or wise or prepared you think you are, this one will blow you out of the water and onto uncharted emotional shores.

The pain is real, the grieving essential. Then, there's the learning, the growing, the rainbow that lies at the far end of the process, the gift hidden in the clouds.

Getting over the double-whammy of 2017 took me a long time. The process involved tears, prayers, a circle of close friends, and dedicated self-care practices. Nature has always been among my best therapists, so I did a lot of outdoor exercise: walking, hiking, swimming, cycling, dancing.

Later that year, still struggling emotionally, I went alone on a month-long walking exploration through the south of France. I channeled my grief into learning a new language and culture, to finding the courage and strength to go forward alone each day, to being receptive to the beauty and wonder, the new sights and sounds. I hiked to exhaustion, falling into bed at the end of each day and then hiking again the next day. I mumbled to myself (who's the crazy lady on the trail?), cried, then cried some more, wrote it all down in my journal, prayed a lot, and called my friends and family for support and love when I felt overwhelmed. Thank heavens for the Internet!

No matter how far away you run, at some point you need to come back and face the situation. Of course, I knew that. But when I did return home, I felt stronger, more resilient. I could breathe again, and I could definitely walk again. One day, I would fly again.

Why do I tell you all this?

So that you will understand my life has not always been a bed of roses,
fame, and fortune, and to share the lesson
I learned from my two lightning strikes:

There will be times when Life makes you **Stop,**
times when you get shocked to your core,
and perhaps you even have burn holes . . .
You will surely need to take time to recover, to heal. To learn. To grow.
But it doesn't mean that you need to stop flying.

CHAPTER 21

When Love is Not Enough

Sometimes love is not enough.

Life happens. Things change, people change, you change. When what you love is hurting you, and you've tried every way you know to fix the situation but it's still not working, at some point you realize that you have to let go. That's why, at the end of 2006, I hung up my wings for the first time, way before normal retirement age. Let me tell you why.

By now, you know how much I loved being a pilot. What changed?

I did. My body did—and so did the demands of the job. Taken together, the two didn't work so well for me anymore. You see, as the airline industry became more competitive over the years, flight crew schedules became more and more demanding. Flying through the night became the norm rather than the exception.

I've never been a night owl. Missing a night's sleep, or most of it, has always been a challenge, even in my partying youth. Anyone who works night-shifts will identify with prep-sleeping during the day to power up for a full night at work, then sleeping most of the next day to recover. The point is that daytime sleep does not provide the same benefits as nighttime sleep. The body doesn't recover or heal as well. Unlike other shift workers, our schedule had no regularity, so our bodies could not develop a pattern for rest and action. Studies show how important our circadian rhythms are for our well-being, and, like many flight crew, mine were constantly being turned upside down. Sometimes I would fly three or four night flights a week. Over time, the erratic schedule began to affect my health.

I noticed, but tried to ignore that my body, once strong, fit, and resilient, was taking longer and longer to bounce back from a red-eye flight. A deep-seated exhaustion would creep in that didn't disappear until I got at least two full nights of rest. I found myself laid low by any little virus that came along, with a simple cold often turning into serious bronchitis.

My husband was the first to voice concern. "Honey, I know you love flying, but do you realize you're getting sick all the time?"

"Oh, no, no, no!" I said, in denial. "I'm just a little tired. I'll be fine."

But I eventually became sick and tired of feeling sick and tired and listened to what my husband and my body were telling me. So, at the end of 2006, I hung up my wings, as I said, for the first time.

For the next two years, I enjoyed a whole different approach to life. How wonderful it was to be able to sleep uninterrupted every night—in my own bed!—not to mention how wonderful it was to enjoy quality time with my husband, dogs, and home. Gradually, I regained my health and resilience.

Never one to sit around doing nothing, I began looking for something fascinating that might fill the void that flying had left, something that might engage and excite me going forward in my new life as a retired pilot.

Then the phone rang. It was Caribbean Airlines (BWIA's successor airline). They needed some extra pilots for a while and invited me back on a short-term contract. My heart leaped. I said I would think about it (think? hah! no need!) and went to find my husband. He saw the joy radiating from me, the spring in my step at the very thought of flying again. So, of course, he gave his blessing.

Oh, the wonder of returning to the airport, to ground school, to simulator training, and finally to flying the skies. The first time I sat in the cockpit, I felt as if I had never left. It was like coming home. I was back where I belonged.

The first few months were wonderful. Then I started to notice that old familiar feeling creeping back. I was becoming chronically tired from so many night flights. I took more vitamins and spent most of my free time at home resting.

Nevertheless, my resistance plummeted, and once again I fell prey to any virus that passed through my airspace. What my body needed was regular deep sleep on a regular nightly basis, and my flying schedule made that impossible. By the end of this contract I was more than ready to retire again. I couldn't wait to return to a life of daytime activity and nighttime rest.

But my heart, the heart of a pilot, was still hooked. So a year later, when the phone call came again, my heart leaped and sang joyously inside me. YES! I raced back to Caribbean Airlines for another contract.

Crazy? Yes. Love can be like that. We go back in the name of love, even when it isn't good for our well-being. Once again, I experienced joy to be back in the cockpit, and once again, after four or five months, the same lingering exhaustion.

The message was clear. My heart still loved flying airplanes, but after so many years of flying, my body was in rebellion against the schedule. To face this realization was difficult, so over the next few years, I answered the call from Caribbean Airlines again and yet again, each time with joy, and each time with the same results to my health.

I actually "retired" four times before I was finally able to let go of flying forever.

But everything ends. Early in 2014, I flew that beautiful B737 jet for the last time—no fanfare, just a quiet departure from a career I loved with all my heart.

Was it hard? Oh, yes.

Do I miss flying a jet? Always. And I always will.

I lived my dream for almost twenty-eight years and loved all those years. But sometimes, even though we don't want to admit it, love is not enough—not if it makes you ill or damages your well-being. This maxim is true in our relationships, and it was true for me with my beloved career.

The time had come to move on, to put health and well-being at the forefront of my life, to create a new beginning.

A Message for You

When something is gone,
Something better is coming.

—Unknown

PART THREE

HUMMINGBIRD
2007-Present (2022)

*There is no purpose for your life greater than to recognize
your own beauty, power and worth and to share it.*

Alan Cohen

CHAPTER 22

Changing the Tyres

P
eople often ask:
What does it feel like to be retired after such an exciting, high-flying life? Aren't you bored? The answer is a resounding NO. I don't do bored. It's not a place I live in.

When I retired from flying, that important part of my life stopped, but *my life* did not. With huge curiosity, I turned my attention to the future.

Whatever could I do with the years ahead?

I wanted to be inspired, excited, and passionate about something new.

It took some doing, some experimentation, but, eventually, I found it.

Let me tell the story as it happened, from the beginning of my first retirement at the start of 2007 . . .

I started my new life as a lady of leisure by settling into a wellness routine. This involved regular outdoor exercise, nature activities, good food, nightly deep sleep (a feature sorely missing in the last few years of my flying career), and quality time with the people I loved most. I soon felt my energy, health, and resilience returning, so I turned my attention to trying new things.

Setting no limitations, I initially explored the world of online trading, but soon decided it was not for me. Then I became a luxury villa manager, learning new skills in marketing, management and maintenance. I became really good at villa management and ran a successful business for years.

> Did it fill my heart? No.
> Pay for groceries and trips? Yes.
> Did I need something more to inspire me? Definitely.

I wanted to do something with my life that would add value to the lives of others, to the world.

I became intrigued by the concept of Feng Shui, an ancient Chinese metaphysical art. Although deep and complex, the simplest way to explain Feng Shui is that it's all about Chi, or energy. Feng Shui is the study of the energy of a space, with the aim of enhancing that energy to support life and well-being.

The more I researched Feng Shui, the more fascinated I became. In 2007, I flew to California for two weeks of intensive training with a renowned Feng Shui master. On my return, I applied the new concepts and principles at home. The effects were felt almost at once, and commented upon by visitors to our home. They knew something had changed even though they couldn't quite identify why the place felt different. This stuff worked!

My interest in wellness also led me to become certified in live blood analysis. I became qualified to assess people's blood and advise them about life-style changes to improve their health. After a year or two,

I found I didn't enjoy spending so much time at a desk looking at the world through a microscope. So I let live blood analysis go and returned my attention to Feng Shui, taking my studies to a higher level. In 2014, after three years of participation in the prestigious BTB Feng Shui Masters Training Program in New York, I became certified as a master-level consultant.

One of the things I love about practicing Feng Shui is that it's like reading a good book in which the reader can make a difference to the outcome. You see, each space tells a story of what is *really* going on in the personal or professional life of a client. For example, a client may request help with relationship challenges, and their home may reveal why those challenges exist. Is the place full of clutter, symbolizing no space in that person's life for another person? Do the images in the home signify loneliness, perhaps holding on to an old love? Is the bedroom a testament to solitude?

With this understanding, I can help clients to shift the *chi*, to break free of whatever has been holding them back from living their best life. It's what I love to do, and why I chose the name Healing Spaces Caribbean for my Feng Shui consultancy.

In my spare time, I hike, swim, read and travel, hang out with friends and loved ones, and explore new worlds through online courses. I also serve on the board of directors of two wonderful non-profit organizations, Yahweh Foundation Tobago and the International Feng Shui Guild, that help to enhance lives and create balance on our beautiful planet.

And . . . I dance. How I dance! The chubby little girl who dreamed of becoming a prima ballerina (but instead became a pilot) has never lost her joy of dancing. Now, in her retirement, she has become quite the Dancing Queen. I may well be the oldest person in my dance school, but I can still shake a leg with the best of them. From lessons to socials to performances and competitions, Latin and ballroom fill my life with sparkle and passion.

Do I miss flying?

Of course I do.

I will love flying forever. After all, it was my original passion, my first ikigai.

What's an ikigai?

An ikigai is the reason you get up in the morning with joy in your heart, ready for action.

An ikigai is what you love to do so much that it doesn't feel like work.

An ikigai fills your days with purpose, your heart with excitement and passion.

Even though I have released my first love, I have found another ikigai. My ikigai is not Feng Shui in itself; it's what I can *do* with it. Feng Shui is my *tool* for helping people understand that everything is energy, and if you can change the energy of a situation, everything can change. I love witnessing that eureka moment when someone really "gets" this concept, the moment when their whole worldview shifts, and they open up to new possibilities. *This* is what excites me, gets me up in the morning with zest and joy, what fires me up.

This is my new ikigai.

For those who worry about retirement, about what to do with all that newfound time, I have joyous news for you.

Retirement doesn't necessarily mean being put out to pasture, being useless, or being bored.

Retirement can mean *changing the tires.*

And—you can choose to change your tires again and again . . .

Once you are blessed with life and health, it's never too late to change direction.

It's your life. Live it!

So, to answer the original question (*what does it feel like to be retired after such an exciting, high-flying life? Aren't you bored?*): No, I am never bored. My life after flying is busy, rich, and full.

I've just changed the tires, that's all.

> ### A Message for You
>
> *Do not go where the path may lead,*
> *go instead where there is no path and leave a trail.*
>
> *The only person you are destined to become*
> *is the person you decide to be.*
>
> — Ralph Waldo Emerson

Still Reaching for the Stars, Dancesport 2018.

Keynote Speaker at Association of Female Executives of
Trinidad and Tobago (AFETT) International Women's Day 2018.

Sharing a laugh with Ms. Charlene Pedro,
former president of AFETT.

CHAPTER 23

And Then Came COVID-19

A nd then, early in 2020, along came COVID-19 . . . and life as we knew it disappeared. One heartless microscopic virus turned the entire world onto its head almost overnight. Fear took over the minds and hearts of many as relationships were torn asunder over different viewpoints about how to handle the crisis. In the face of so much illness, so many deaths, the lives of people everywhere were changed forever.

None of the plans, expectations, hopes or dreams that previously fired up our lives were possible, or valid, in the "new normal." There seemed no end in sight, and many despaired of ever regaining some semblance of normalcy in their lives.

From my Feng Shui point of view, the energy of the world changed abruptly from exciting and expansive to fearful and constricted. Everywhere life seemed full of shadows, and the future looked bleak. Would there ever be a return to freedom, to joy, laughter, and light?

In 2022, with the virus reducing in virulence, many restrictions were eased to allow economies and people to start the long journey back to normal. The response from the population was to celebrate their new freedoms, with the unsurprising result: infections soared, even though the symptoms were not as severe or deadly as before.

That's when I got the dreaded bug. After staying safe and healthy (and locked down) for more than two years, I went dancing. Two years without much social contact, not to mention without dancing, had seemed so long! Ahhh, the sheer joy of it! However, a few days later, I noticed tell-tale signs that I was coming down with a flu. I was tested, and the news was no surprise: Positive for COVID-19. That delightful night of dancing had been costly.

Even though I normally feel and look years younger than my biological age, the fact is, I am a senior citizen with a history of previous lung conditions (bronchitis and pneumonia), so I was considered high risk for complications. Testing positive for the corona virus was terrible news.

Two weeks of aches and pains, night sweats, weakness, and chest congestion brought me to the other side, with the only lingering impact a deep-seated exhaustion. Apparently, this high-energy retired pilot had met her match in COVID-19; I no longer had any desire to hike up a mountain before breakfast. The idea that I would one day be able to return to my accustomed activity level seemed like a distant pipe dream.

But, like dark nights of the soul often do, my brush with COVID-19 brought its own hidden gifts. That's something that I've learned over my lifetime: that no matter how bad things may feel and look, a gift is always hidden somewhere in its dark folds.

What were the gifts of COVID-19?
During the long months of lockdown, when people were forced to live and work from home and give up non-essential social contact, I learned:
> how much I love the people whom I love;
> how important it is to stay connected, to *be* connected;
> how to be happy (not just satisfied) with my own company, with my own home, and my own life.

Like people everywhere, I also had to make changes to my accustomed ways of living life, and I learned that those changes brought unexpected benefits. Here are just a few . . .

- Because of lockdowns, travel wasn't possible for a long while. One might think this would bother me, a dedicated adventure traveler. Not at all! Given the state of the world I had no desire whatsoever to travel. Instead, once movement was allowed, I set out to explore more fully the nooks and crannies of my own country and found places of unbelievable beauty that I had not previously noticed.

- Unable to visit my Feng Shui clients, or offer in-person workshops as I loved to do, I was forced to shift my consultancy online. That involved learning new skills: how to use Zoom like a professional, how to teach effectively online, how to offer impactful virtual consultations. In a very short time I became as proficient in helping my clients through the ether as I had been in person. There were so many benefits: now I could help people all over the world to change their lives through distance consultations, interactive online workshops, and private mentoring sessions. By locking us all down, COVID-19 actually pushed me to open up my world.

- To be effective online, I also had to expand my horizons on social media, something I had always avoided. "Keep my head down" had always been my motto on Facebook! Now, here I was taking courses to strengthen my online marketing and social media skills. I'm much more confident now in cyberspace; I manage a chi-lifting Facebook group, offer live events and virtual trainings, participate in interviews, podcasts and summits with people across the globe. All because of COVID-19!

Then in 2022, came the sobering experience of my actually being sick with COVID-19. I can't say that was fun in any way! As I write this, I am still in recovery mode, every day becoming a little stronger. I am now able to reflect on the hidden gifts of the past two weeks of physical misery, these realizations (I should really call them reminders, because deep inside I've known them all along):

I am loved. So many people came forward to help me when I felt as helpless as a kitten. I am hugely grateful for the outpouring of love and support.

My never-ending to-do list, which seems so essential when I feel well, became irrelevant when I was faced with a major battle for my health.

Breathing is the single most important activity that has to be done, every instant, of every day.

Everything else is optional.

I am in love with life. When I return to full well-being, I intend to treasure and honor the life I have with every breath, every word, every action

Thank you, Covid.

A Message for You

A man who is well wants one thousand things.
A man who is sick wants only one thing.

Old Chinese Proverb

No matter what happens, there is always a hidden gift.
Always.

EPILOGUE

_____

The Courage to Fly

People tend to judge books by their cover. It's easy to look from the outside at someone whose life appears to be better than yours and feel a touch of envy, to think *probably she was lucky and had all the breaks*.

We can never know another's journey unless we have walked in that person's boots.
The only boots we can really know are our own boots.

I *do* feel my life has been a wonderful adventure, and I have been blessed—

But I have had to work for every single blessing, not only by putting in the physical and mental effort to achieve my goals but also by conquering the inner voices of fear and doubt and limiting beliefs that often rose up and shouted at me.

The inner work has always been the biggest challenge. I've had to learn not to be influenced by other people's opinions, to listen instead to my heart, the whispers of my soul. I've had to be willing to learn and to give up old paradigms and some unhelpful habits. I've had to find the courage to face my fears, to walk alone into the unknown, trusting that I would be Divinely guided with every trembling step. In this scary, changing world of ours, that takes a lot of trust.

My journey was not always easy or smooth. I have experienced financial challenges, personal loss, heartbreaking grief, life-threatening illness. At times, life knocked me down so hard I couldn't imagine I would be ever able to get up and walk again, let alone fly again.

But I did. It took time and courage and support from my inner circle, but I did.

As I write this book, I am sixty-seven years old. In the eyes of the world I am a senior citizen—an old lady, even—but I don't feel old. I feel full, and excited, and alive.

I'm blessed to be healthy, to be able to dance and hike with the best of them. I'm still curious, eager to learn and grow. I am currently involved in three courses, each bringing different new skills and understanding. One of these courses will teach me how to publish and promote this book, and since you're reading it, I guess I finished the course!

I look forward to the next chapter of my life: to new wisdom, to lots more dancing, and many more adventures. On my bucket list is a flight into outer space. I've always dreamed of seeing our beautiful planet Earth from higher than 37,000 feet! That must surely be magical, as close to heaven as I can get while still alive.

But what about *you*? Have I helped *you* believe?

Do you understand that you are a unique, special, God-given energy residing in a human body, capable of things of which you never dreamed? You are, literally, a Force of Nature!

The challenge is to believe—to disregard all the so-called evidence around you and tap into the Divine spark that lives within, whatever your spiritual belief system might be; to know that as long as you are here, there is a reason for your life, a reason why you continue to breathe in . . . and breathe out. Something of value exists for you to do, and that value is not defined by the outer world. It is defined by your inner world. It doesn't matter if the outside world has other ideas about who you should be or what you should do with your life. Listen to the voice in your heart, then follow it with every fiber of your being.

I truly hope that my story has inspired you to live the life you were meant to live, to become the human being that only *you* can be. Fearlessly.

I leave you with these thoughts

Live your own life. No one else can live it for you.
Yes, you **Can.**
It's never too late to learn, to grow, to change your path.
There is no shame in trying something and deciding that it's not for you.
But if you don't try, you will never know.
Everything in your life experience depends on the energy you bring to it.
Everyone needs an ikigai. It lives in your heart. Just listen.
Reach for the stars. Even if you fall, you might just land on the moon.
Always be the best human being you can be.
Love. BIG.
Dare to Dream. BIG.
and . . .
Have the Courage to Fly.

With love, and with faith in you,

ONE LAST MESSAGE

CONGRATULATIONS!

I am so proud of you for making the great decision to read this book, all the way to the very end.

It means you really have a strong desire to follow those dreams of yours, all the way to the end of the rainbow.

My mission with this book has been to inspire you to believe in yourself, to chase those rainbows, no matter what challenges you may face, and no matter what the world may be telling you.

I hope that you have been both inspired, and empowered . . . to DO more, BE more, and ACHIEVE more . . . than you ever thought possible.

I hope you have found within yourself: The COURAGE TO FLY.

"Dare to live the life you have dreamed for yourself.
Go forward and make your dreams come true."

— Ralph Waldo Emerson

ACKNOWLEDGMENTS

Through the years, many people have blessed me with their ideas, mentoring and support, each person impacting my life in a different, meaningful way. It's impossible to thank everyone and I apologise for anyone not listed. Please know that I appreciate you greatly.

In no particular order: I am hugely grateful to Fareeda Hosein, Jeanne Mason for the production and editing of this book; to my special wingmen Marjorie Linglet and Terri Osborne, for your unfailingly honest feedback, keen insight and unwavering support. I thank Katinka Kundler, Elspeth Duncan, Arlene Navarro, Michael J. Keens-Dumas, Vidya Lall, Gale Corbie, and Shannon Hutchinson for encouraging me and believing in this book.

For pushing me out of my social media comfort zone, I thank Judette Coward; I also thank James Mallinchuk, Nick and Megan Unsworth, Tony Robbins and Dean Graziosi: Your trainings gave me the courage, and the tools, to take my message to the world.

To my family, I couldn't have become the person that I did, without you. Thank you from my heart.

ABOUT WENDY

Wendy Yawching was the first female Captain of T&T's national airline, the first Trinidadian woman to hike the trail to Mt Everest Base Camp, and the first Master Feng Shui consultant in T&T.

Wendy is a powerful **inspirational speaker**, particularly at youth & women's forums. Her mission is to inspire and empower women and girls everywhere, especially those in situations where dreams do not typically flourish.

She can speak worldwide, virtually or in-person, to groups of all sizes.

www.speaker.theCourage2Fly.com

Wendy is the **coach/mentor** of choice for girls and women who wish to shake off the limiting mental/emotional chains that bind them and reach for the stars.

www.mentor.theCourage2Fly.com

As a Master Feng Shui Consultant, Wendy is uniquely positioned to help you create home and business spaces that support your dreams and your life. Learn more about her services and workshop offerings here:

www.HealingSpacesCaribbean.com

Special FREE Bonus Gift for You

To help you to fly even higher, there are
FREE BONUS RESOURCES
for you at:
www.FreeGift.theCourage2Fly.com

* Free TheCourage2Fly e-workbook/journal
Special Discount & VIP upgrade to Wendy's signature
transformational workshop, *New Beginnings:*
The Ultimate Energy Vision Board Experience

ADDITIONAL RESOURCES
NEW BEGINNINGS:
THE ULTIMATE ENERGY VISION BOARD EXPERIENCE

Revision Your Life with Wendy's transformational Energy Vision Board process.
There is no other vision board program like this one.
Step forward into your greatness!

Www.Newbeginnings.healingspacescaribbean.com

HANG OUT WITH WENDY
Inner Circle Mentoring

Let Wendy walk beside you as you journey into your best future.

www.mentor.theCourage2Fly.com

You can live as if nothing is a miracle, or
You can live as if everything is a miracle.
——Albert Einstein

Photo: F. Hosein

Printed in Great Britain
by Amazon

33206180R00077